OVERNIGHT CAREER CHOICE

discover your ideal job in just a few hours

MICHAEL FARR

Also in JIST's Help in a Hurry Series

Same-Day Resume

Next-Day Job Interview

15-Minute Cover Letter

Seven-Step Job Search

JIST
Works
America's Career Publisher

PART OF JIST'S HELP IN A HURRY™ SERIES

OVERNIGHT CAREER CHOICE

© 2006 by JIST Publishing, Inc.

Published by JIST Works, an imprint of JIST Publishing, Inc.
8902 Otis Avenue
Indianapolis, IN 46216-1033
Phone: 1-800-648-JIST   Fax: 1-800-JIST-FAX   E-mail: info@jist.com

Visit our Web site at **www.jist.com** for information on JIST, book excerpts, and ordering information on our many products. For free information on 14,000 job titles, visit **www.careeroink.com.**

Quantity discounts are available for JIST books. Please call our Sales Department at 1-800-648-JIST or visit www.jist.com for a free catalog and more information.

Acquisitions and Development Editor: Susan Pines
Database Work: Laurence Shatkin
Interior Designer and Layout Technician: Aleata Howard
Cover Designer: Katy Bodenmiller
Proofreader: Linda Seifert
Indexer: Kelly D. Henthorne

Printed in the United States of America

10 09 08 07 06 05   9 8 7 6 5 4 3 2 1

Library of Congress Cataloging-in-Publication Data

Farr, J. Michael.
    Overnight career choice : discover your ideal job in just a few hours / Michael Farr.
        p. cm. -- (JIST's help in a hurry series)
    Includes index.
    ISBN 1-59357-252-2 (alk. paper)
1. Vocational interests. 2. Vocational qualifications. 3. Job satisfaction. I. Title. II. Series.
    HF5381.5.F37 2006
    650.14--dc22

                                                        2005027205

ISBN 1-59357-252-2

Choose Your Ideal Career Tonight

This small book is designed to quickly make a big difference in your career and your life by helping you discover your career focus.

Many people spend months or years unhappy in their careers. Some move from job to job, always searching for more-fulfilling or better-paying work. Others say they "fell into" a career without asking if it suited them. Still others follow in the footsteps of a parent, take any available job, or pursue a hot new field. These paths work out for some people, of course. But many others never discover their true career interests and are dissatisfied with work.

According to research, most people can expect three to five career changes during their working years and ten or more job changes. In addition, only half of all workers are happy with their jobs. These indicators show a clear need for more careful career planning both now and throughout our working lives.

Fortunately, through a proven process and some current facts on jobs, this book helps you pinpoint your ideal career without wasting time and energy. Is it that easy and quick to find your career fit? The answer is "Yes!" This book shows you how. Start with the introduction for guidance in getting the most from this book in a short time.

I wish you well in your career and your life.

Contents

A Brief Introduction to Using This Book

If you are going to work, you might as well do something you enjoy, are good at, and want to do. Yet many people struggle with finding their career focus.

I assume that you are ready for a career change or maybe your first career. Perhaps you can't seem to find the right job, have lost your job, or want more meaningful work. You could, through trial and error, learn which career suits you best. You could read longer books on the topic. You could take a career interest inventory or other test to narrow your options. While these efforts may be helpful, they take time, money, and energy. None is guaranteed to give you the insight you need to make a good career choice. Career choice is a complex decision, as I explain in Chapter 1.

Follow a Proven Process for Making a Good Career Choice

Fortunately, a proven process for discovering your ideal career exists. This book, in a short period of time, takes you through the key steps in this process. When you finish this book, you will have spent more time planning your career than most people do in a lifetime.

So I applaud you for picking up this book and for deciding to learn more about your career options. The time you spend is very likely to pay off in career success and satisfaction for years to come.

You Don't Have to Read All Night

You can get through this book by working through it today as I suggest below, sleeping on what you learn, and finishing up tomorrow. (You don't need to stay up all night unless you want to!) Just follow this roadmap to get the most from this book:

1. **Read the table of contents.** It introduces you to the content of the book and its chapters.

2. **Learn the most important points about career choice by skimming Chapter 1.** Read the opening paragraphs and the sections that sound most interesting to you in Chapter 1. Pay special attention to the section called "The Nine Most Important Components of an Ideal Job." You can read the entire chapter in detail later if you wish.

3. **Gain insight into your key skills by completing the checklists and worksheets in Chapter 2.** This chapter may take more time to get through than the other chapters will. But the results are worth it because knowing what you are good at is an essential part of choosing a career. Unless you use the skills you enjoy and are good at, it is unlikely you will be fully satisfied in your career.

4. **Discover what interests you most by reviewing the 16 career interest areas described in Chapter 3.** Identify the career clusters that interest you most. This step helps you more clearly identify specific careers to consider in Chapter 6.

5. **Consider your key work values and motivators in Chapter 4.** This short chapter presents a checklist of values that give people the most satisfaction and success. Work values include creativity, stability, independence, good pay, good coworkers, and a sense of accomplishment.

6. **Review six other factors important in your ideal career in Chapter 5.** These factors include preferred earnings, level of responsibility desired, preferred location, special knowledge that you would like to use in your career, desired work environment, and the types of people you would like to work with and for.

7. **Review major job titles and job descriptions for your key career interest areas.** Chapter 6 is lengthy, but you don't need to read it all. Instead, under your top career interest areas (identified in Chapter 3) skim the jobs and check those that sound most interesting.

8. **Pinpoint the industries that interest you the most in Chapter 7.** The industry you work in is often as important as what job you choose because of pay, stability, your interest in it, and other factors. Use the checklist in this chapter to learn which industries suit you best.

9. **Put your ideal career choice into words in Chapter 8.** Focus on completing the "Overnight Career Choice Matrix" and the "Your Ideal Job Definition."

By following the preceding suggestions, you will target the most important questions in career choice, get to know yourself a little better, and clearly define your career focus. Chapter 9 helps you write your job objective when you're ready to begin your job search.

So what are you waiting for? Jump right in and find your career focus!

© JIST Works

Chapter 1

Quick But Important Points About Career Choice

People often approach career choice with the assumption that they are looking for a particular job title. This is a sensible approach, and this book helps you pinpoint the job titles that suit you best. But this book also helps you consider other factors, in addition to a job title, to help you define your *ideal* job.

For example, what interests do you have, what industry would you like to work in, with what sorts of people, and in what sort of an organization? The answers to these and other questions can be *very* important to you for a variety of reasons yet often are not given much consideration.

This chapter introduces the nine most important factors to consider in defining your ideal job. It also helps you explore the role that education and training plays in your career choice. Chapter 6 helps you research specific job titles that match your current or future needs and wishes.

Defining Your "Ideal" Job Is Tricky

Defining your ideal job is tricky business. The U.S. Department of Labor has formal written descriptions for thousands of job titles. This is far too many jobs for anyone to know well enough to consider. Add to that the many substantial differences among employers and work environments, and the choices quickly become overwhelming. You might be delighted to work in one place and miserable working in another. Yet, both jobs could have the same job title and look much the same on paper.

Many people confuse their ideal job with a job title, but they are not the same thing at all. For example, if you were looking for a job as a sales-person, computer technician, chef, or teacher, those are job titles. Your ideal job, however, is more complex and specific to you and your needs.

Clarifying What You Want to Do Involves More Than Choosing a Job Title

Most people don't take the time to clarify what they have to offer or what they want to do. They stick to a job similar to one they had in the past or that is related to their education or training. Rather than analyze what they really want to do, they pursue what they believe they are qualified for. I have seen many people choose a job title and then put it on their resume or job applications as their job objective.

While your ideal job and your job objective are not exactly the same thing, I want to talk a little about job objectives because most people are familiar with them. In addition, a well-done job objective contains many elements that are similar to an ideal career definition.

> **Note:** *A job objective focuses on what you can do for the employer. Your ideal career definition covers similar points but includes the things that you want, such as good pay, a short commute, and friendly coworkers. I cover job objectives in detail in Chapter 9.*

Here is an example of a nicely written job objective from someone's resume: "A position requiring skills in organizing, communicating, and dealing with people. Prefer a small- to mid-size organization engaged in creative activities. Background in office management. Skilled in word processing, spreadsheets, Internet research, and other computer operations."

Although it doesn't mention a job title, this is just the sort of thing that a person who has worked as an administrative assistant or other office position might write on a resume. It mentions skills and preferences without limiting job choices.

This approach leaves open a variety of options that would not be called administrative assistant, and it also provides more information on what the person wants and is good at doing. This sample job objective would allow this person to do a wide variety of jobs and not be limited to a specific job called administrative assistant. Other jobs this person might do include

- Office manager
- Sales associate

- Customer service representative

- Receptionist

- Researcher

- Human resources assistant

- Web site coordinator

> **Tip:** *A good career choice involves more than deciding on a job title. For example, if you have training in accounting but have great interest in fashion design, can you think of a career that might combine these two things? Or what if you are a computer repair technician but also enjoy selling? The fact is that you can combine these things—and other factors important to you—in a job.*

Many people show a lack of clarity in their search for a job by seeking a job title, rather than the type of work, employer, and work environment they prefer. As a result, they often end up being an accountant (or whatever) instead of doing something they really want to do.

So don't limit yourself now by choosing just a job title or later by listing an option-killing job title on your resume. Instead, be clear about what you want and have to offer and seek an employer who will allow you to do a job that fits those interests and skills.

Most People Want More Than Money from Work

For most of human history, a high percentage of people were not happy in their jobs. Of course, back then, many people didn't expect to be happy in their work. Work was, well, work, and what enjoyment you had was likely to come from outside of work.

However, more people now look for both meaning and enjoyment from the way they earn their livings. While many people still go to work simply to earn a paycheck, many want more. According to a recent survey by the Conference Board, a New York-based business research group, half of all Americans are unhappy with their jobs.

Most people rate various measures of personal satisfaction very high in their jobs. The type of work you do and the people you work with are consistently more important to your job satisfaction than pay. In addition, you are more likely to enjoy, stay in, and be successful at a career that suits your interests and skills. For these reasons, you would be wise to spend some time considering what you want out of your work.

Money Is Important, But Other Things Are More Important

A study by the Gallup Poll indicated that 78 percent of those surveyed rated "interesting work" as very important in being satisfied with their jobs. Only one measure, "good health insurance and other benefits," was rated higher. While many people value making good money (particularly if you don't make enough to live reasonably well), only 56 percent rated "high income" as being very important to them. It's not that money isn't important. It's just that most working people value other things, too. The table that follows shows other things that were rated higher than money:

What Makes People Satisfied with Their Jobs

Factor	Percentage of People Rating as Important
Good health insurance and other benefits	80
Interesting work	78
Job security	78
Opportunity to learn new skills	68
Having a week or more of vacation	66
Being able to work independently	64
Recognition from coworkers	62
Regular hours, no weekends or nights	58
Being able to help others	58
Limiting job stress	58
High income	56

The next table shows the results of another survey, this one by Louis Harris and Associates, asking people to rate those things they considered to be very important in their work. Again, money comes up as important, but not as important as some other things.

What People Say Is Very Important in Their Work

Factor	Percentage of People Rating as Important
A challenging job	82
Good benefits	80
Good pay	74

Factor	Percentage of People Rating as Important
Free exchange of information	74
Chance to make significant contributions	74
The right to privacy	62

The final table presents the results of a survey taken by Research & Forecasts. It asked people to rate various work factors and select their two most important choices. The percentages indicate those who selected each item among their highest two work-related values. It makes sense that those with lower levels of education rate money as most important, because they are likely to earn less than those with more education. But more than 50 percent of the high school graduates or those with less education picked other things as more important than pay alone.

Work Values Differ by Level of Education

Factor	High School Graduate or Less	Some College	College Graduate
Percent selecting factor among two most important			
Pay	46	42	29
Amount of independence	31	35	40
Pleasant working conditions	30	23	17
Liking the people at work	29	24	19
Gratifying work	25	32	43
Contribution to the public good	11	14	23
Important career step	10	15	19

The Nine Most Important Components of an Ideal Job

Many experts have given a lot of thought to the factors a person should consider in selecting a job that is particularly well suited to them. A large body of research provides predictors for career satisfaction and success,

Tip: *Most people don't think about the following factors in an organized way. Yet, these very things help you find your true career focus and make a huge difference in your long-term career satisfaction and success.*

with great differences in opinion on what approach is most valid or which factors most important to consider when making a career choice.

I have identified nine factors that play a key role in defining your ideal job. I have adapted these factors or steps from what vocational researchers suggest are the most important things to consider in defining your ideal career.

Nine Key Factors to Consider in Planning Your Career

1. Skills and abilities
2. Interests
3. Personal values
4. Preferred earnings
5. Level of responsibility
6. Location
7. Special knowledge
8. Work environment
9. Types of people you like to work with and for

You may have noticed that what is not included in the list is a job title. That can come later, after the other factors are clearly defined.

Chapters that follow help you pinpoint the characteristics of your ideal job by exploring what you really want in terms of your interests, values, skills, and other preferences. In addition, 275 brief job descriptions and 40 industry descriptions help you further explore possible career options.

The Role of Education and Training in Career Choice

Too many people think that once they finish their formal education, they are set for life. Not so. No matter how much education or training you have, you may need more to change, advance, and succeed in your career. Even if you stay in your current field and just fine-tune your career focus, you most likely will need training to keep up with changes in technology, to increase your productivity, to upgrade your skills, and to get promoted.

While a new career choice may send you back to school, don't let the need for more education hold you back from your ideal job. With the many education and training options available today, including short-term certificate programs, online learning, night school, internships, learning through volunteer work, and accelerated programs, you can be on your way to a new career sooner than you may think.

Education and Earnings Are Closely Related

Although earnings are not the most important thing to most workers, your salary affects your life. But higher-paying jobs require higher-level skills and more training and education.

While there is a clear relationship between level of education and earnings, most people don't realize how substantial the differences are as the education level of an individual increases. Following are the earnings by level of education as released by the U.S. Department of Labor. I calculated the dollar and percent premium of pay over those who dropped out of high school.

Annual Earnings for Full-Time Workers Ages 25 and Older, by Educational Attainment			
Education Level	Earnings Per Year	Earnings Premium Over High School Dropouts	Percent Earnings Over High School Dropouts
Some high school, no diploma	$21,400		
High school diploma/GED	$28,800	$7,400	35
Some college, no degree	$32,400	$11,000	51
Associate degree	$35,400	$14,000	65
Bachelor's degree	$46,300	$24,900	116
Master's degree	$55,300	$33,900	158
Doctorate	$70,500	$49,100	229
Professional degree	$80,200	$58,800	275

When you look at the numbers, it's clear that additional education pays off at all levels. A high school graduate earns $7,400 or 35 percent more than the average high school dropout. A four-year college graduate earns almost $17,500 more than a high school graduate. This means that, over a decade, a college graduate will earn about $175,000 more than someone with a high school diploma. That is enough to make a big difference in lifestyle and more than enough to pay off any cost of the education itself. Over a 40-year work life, the difference in earnings is staggering. The average college graduate will earn well over a million dollars more than a high school graduate, after inflation is considered.

More Education Does Not Guarantee Success

Most people earn more as they increase their level of education or training, but success is not guaranteed. This is particularly true for those entering the job market with new credentials. For example, the outlook for those with four-year college degrees is quite good, with jobs requiring this degree projected to grow faster than the average for all jobs, according to the U.S. Department of Labor.

While the long-term projections for college graduates are quite good, there are other things to consider to fully understand these projections. For one thing, about 20 percent of the college graduates in the workforce are either unemployed (about 3 percent) or are holding jobs not typically held by college grads (about 17 percent). Some of those counted as "underemployed" choose to be so while they attend graduate school or spend their time in other ways, but many were unable to find better jobs due to competition or other factors.

> **Note:** *Average earnings can be misleading, because half earn more and half earn less than the average. Also, some high school dropouts earn much more than the average for college graduates.*

The average growth rate for all occupations is projected to be 15 percent (the average growth rate for workers is projected at 12 percent). What is most significant is that all jobs requiring postsecondary training or education are projected to grow more rapidly than average, and all jobs requiring less education are projected to grow more slowly than average.

The bottom line is that while a college degree has great value, it does not guarantee success in the job market. About one in five new grads initially has to accept a job that is not typically held by grads. Eventually, more than 90 percent of new graduates find jobs typically held by college graduates.

All of this information reinforces my observation that career planning is more important than ever.

Trade and Technical Training Are Alternatives to a Four-Year College Degree

> **Tip:** *While have a college degree is clearly a good thing, jobs requiring a two-year associate degree are growing the fastest of all, and many of these jobs are in high-wage medical and technical areas.*

More education clearly pays off in the job market, but it should be noted that college is not the only route to higher earnings. Many trade, technical, sales, and other fields offer similar opportunities to those without a college degree. A well-trained plumber, auto mechanic, chef, computer repair technician, police officer, tool and die maker, or medical technologist can do quite well in our economy.

These and many other occupations require one to two years of specialized training, and many apprenticeship programs allow for on-the-job training while paying you wages. Outstanding people in sales, small business, management, self-employment, and other activities can still do quite well without a college degree, although more education is often required to compete for the better positions.

Many jobs will continue to become available in occupations that are growing slowly or even declining. Jobs will become available to replace those who retire or leave for other reasons, and opportunities will exist in virtually all areas for those with superior abilities, motivation, and preparation.

Career Choice Is a Lifelong Process

No matter how much career planning you do, your career choice will most likely change over the course of your life. Some experts estimate that the average person will change careers three to five times and change jobs ten or more times during their working years.

That is a lot of change, which makes it important for you to know what you are particularly good at doing and develop those skills throughout your life. As your interests change, you may choose to develop new skills or emphasize existing ones in different ways. As you do, look for ways to emphasize your strengths and present them in new and creative ways.

Career Change Versus Job Change

A career change is a change in the type of work you do. While a job change involves moving from one employer to another—and doing a similar job for both—a career change is a more substantial change.

If you waited on tables in a restaurant when going to school, and then got a job as a medical technician when you graduated, that would be a change in career (as well as a change in employer, of course). A career change is when you change your work from one occupational group to another, such as when a teacher leaves the educational system and becomes a real estate agent.

You will never be finished with your career planning, and you probably will need to keep revising your plans as you learn and experience more. This book helps you develop the skills to make the best career choices throughout your life.

Incorporate Life Planning into Your Career Choice

Your current priority may be to find a new or better career. That is a worthy objective. Before you begin the search for your ideal career, however, define clearly what you want and need from a job. Be certain to consider how that job might help you get where you want to go with your life.

Look for Some Meaning in Your Work

Good career planning is extremely important, but it should be done in the context of what you want to do with your life. How can you, for example, incorporate elements of pleasure and learning into your next job?

Earning a living can be a difficult task. Over the years I have done many things that I did not enjoy but did them anyway so that I could "earn a living." What I have learned is that having fun, having meaningful relationships, and finding satisfaction and meaning from what we do with our lives is what life is all about. So look for joy in your life and your job and for some meaning in your life's work.

I hope I have presented a few points in this chapter that help you discover your ideal job. I know there is a lot to think about, and it may seem a bit overwhelming to make a decision to go in one career direction over another. But the stakes are very high for you, both in money and in personal satisfaction.

Key Points: Chapter 1

- Defining your ideal career involves more than just choosing a job title.

- You are more likely to enjoy, stay in, and be successful at a career that suits your interests and skills.

- Nine factors are important when defining your ideal job: skills and abilities, interests, personal values, preferred earnings, level of responsibility, location, special knowledge, work environment, and types of people you like to work with and for.

- Education and training usually play an important role in future earnings.

- Career planning is a lifelong process, and your career choice may change several times as you do.

Chapter 2

What Are You Good At?

The first key factor or step in defining your ideal career is knowing your best skills and abilities. This chapter helps you identify the skills you have and begin to develop a "skills language" that is tremendously important for your career choice, your job search and, more importantly, your life.

Knowing what you are good at is an essential part of choosing a career. Unless you use the skills that you enjoy using and are good at, it is unlikely that you will be fully satisfied in your job.

Most people are not good at recognizing and listing the skills they have. I can tell you this based on many years of working with job seekers. When asked, few people can quickly tell me what they are good at, and fewer still can quickly present the specific skills that are needed to succeed in the job they want.

Many employers also note that most job seekers don't present their skills effectively. According to one survey of employers, more than 90 percent of the people they interview cannot adequately define the skills they have that support their ability to do the job. They may have the necessary skills, but they can't communicate that fact.

Learn the Three Types of Skills

Many people don't realize that everyone has hundreds of skills, not just a few. When I ask someone in a job search workshop what skills they have, too often they say, "I can't think of any."

Simple skills such as closing your fingers to grip a pen (which is not simple at all if you consider the miracle of complex neuromuscular interactions that sophisticated robots can only approximate) are building blocks for more complex skills, such as writing a sentence, and even more complex skills, such as writing a book.

Even though you have hundreds of skills, some will be more important to an employer than others. Some will be far more important to you in deciding what sort of job you want. To simplify the task of skill identification,

I have found it useful to think of skills in the three major categories: adaptive skills, transferable skills, and job-related skills.

Adaptive Skills/Personality Traits

You probably take for granted the many skills you use every day to survive and function. I call these skills *adaptive* or *self-management skills* because they allow you to adapt or adjust to a variety of situations. Some of them could be considered part of your basic personality. Such skills, which are highly valued by employers, include getting to work on time, honesty, enthusiasm, and getting along with others.

Transferable Skills

Transferable skills are general skills that can be useful in a variety of jobs. For example, writing clearly, good language skills, and the ability to organize and prioritize tasks would be desirable skills in many jobs. These skills are called *transferable skills* because they can be transferred from one job—or even one career—to another.

Job-Related Skills

These are the skills people typically think of first when asked, "Do you have any skills?" They are related to a particular job or type of job. An auto mechanic, for example, needs to know how to tune engines and repair brakes. Other jobs also have job-specific skills required for that job in addition to the adaptive and transferable skills needed to succeed in almost any job.

Identify Your Skills

Because being aware of your skills is so important, I include a series of checklists and other activities in this chapter to help you identify your key skills. Recognizing these skills is important so that you select jobs that you will do well in. Developing a skills language can also be very helpful to you in writing resumes and conducting your job search. To begin, answer the question in the box on the next page.

Note: *This system of dividing skills into three categories is not perfect. Some things, such as being trustworthy, dependable, and well-organized, are really not skills as much as they are personality traits that can be acquired. There is also some overlap between the three skills categories. For example, a skill such as being organized might be considered either adaptive or transferable.*

WHAT MAKES YOU A GOOD WORKER?

On the following lines, list three things about yourself that you think make you a good worker. Take your time. Think about what an employer might like about you or the way you work.

1. _____

2. _____

3. _____

The skills you just wrote down may be among the most important things to consider in your career choice. They may also be among the most important things that employers will want to know about you. Most (but not all) people write adaptive skills when asked this question.

Identify Your Adaptive Skills and Personality Traits

I have created a list of adaptive skills that that tend to be important when defining a person's ideal career as well as being important to employers. The ones listed as "The Minimum" are those that most employers consider essential for job survival, and many will not hire someone who has problems in these areas.

Look over the list and put a check mark next to each adaptive skill that you possess. Put a second check mark next to those skills that are particularly important for you to use or include in your next job.

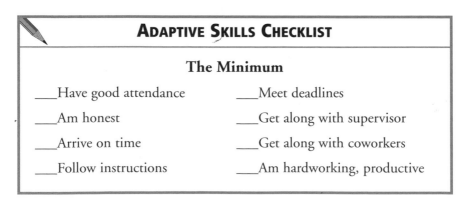

ADAPTIVE SKILLS CHECKLIST

The Minimum

___Have good attendance   ___Meet deadlines

___Am honest   ___Get along with supervisor

___Arrive on time   ___Get along with coworkers

___Follow instructions   ___Am hardworking, productive

Other Adaptive Skills

___Able to coordinate   ___Intuitive   ___Solve problems

___Results-oriented   ___Decisive   ___Team player

___Mentor others   ___Work well with diversity   ___Multitask

___Friendly   ___Discreet   ___Patient

___Ambitious   ___Learn quickly   ___Spontaneous

___Good-natured   ___Eager   ___Persistent

___Assertive   ___Loyal   ___Steady

___Helpful   ___Efficient   ___Physically strong

___Capable   ___Mature   ___Tactful

___Humble   ___Energetic   ___Practical

___Cheerful   ___Methodical   ___Take pride in work

___Imaginative   ___Enthusiastic   ___Competent

___Modest   ___Reliable   ___Independent

___Expressive   ___Tenacious   ___Well organized

___Motivated   ___Resourceful   ___Industrious

___Flexible   ___Thrifty   ___Natural

___Responsible   ___Conscientious   ___Formal

___Trustworthy   ___Informal   ___Open-minded

___Self-confident   ___Creative   ___Optimistic

___Versatile   ___Intelligent   ___Sincere

___Sense of humor   ___Dependable   ___Original

(continued)

(continued)

Other Adaptive Skills You Have

Add any adaptive skills that were not listed but that you think are important on the job:

_____

_____

_____

_____

_____

_____

Your Top Adaptive Skills

Carefully review the checklist you just completed and select the three adaptive skills that you most want to use in your next job. These three skills are *extremely* important to include in your ideal career choice, on your resume, and in job interviews.

1. _____

2. _____

3. _____

Identify Your Transferable Skills

Over the years, I have assembled a list of transferable skills that are important in a wide variety of jobs. In the checklist that follows, I consider the skills listed as "Key Transferable Skills" to be most important for success on the job. The key skills are also those that are often required in jobs with more responsibility and higher pay, so you should emphasize these skills if you have them.

The remaining transferable skills are grouped into categories that may be helpful to you. Go ahead and check each skill you are strong in, and then double-check the skills you want to use in your next job. When you are finished, you should have checked 10 to 20 skills at least once.

TRANSFERABLE SKILLS CHECKLIST

Key Transferable Skills

___Meet deadlines

___Plan

___Speak in public

___Control budgets

___Meet the public

___Negotiate

___Instruct others

___Organize or manage projects

___Solve problems

___Manage money or budgets

___Manage people

___Supervise others

___Increase sales or efficiency

___Accept responsibility

___Write

___Use computers or other technology

Other Transferable Skills

___Drive or operate vehicles

___Build, observe, inspect things

___Assemble or make things

___Construct or repair buildings

Dealing with Data

___Analyze data or facts

___Investigate

___Audit records

___Keep financial records

___Budget

___Locate answers or information

___Calculate, compute

___Manage money

___Classify data

___Negotiate

___Compare, inspect, or record facts

___Count, observe, compile

___Research

___Pay attention to detail

___Use technology to analyze data

___Evaluate

___Take inventory

___Synthesize

(continued)

(continued)

Working with People

___Administer   ___Be pleasant   ___Be diplomatic

___Patient   ___Counsel people   ___Supervise

___Care for others   ___Be sensitive   ___Help others

___Persuade   ___Demonstrate   ___Be tactful

___Confront others   ___Sociable   ___Have insight

___Teach   ___Be tough   ___Understand

___Interview others   ___Listen   ___Be outgoing

___Be tolerant   ___Trust   ___Be kind

___Negotiate

Using Words, Ideas

___Be articulate   ___Correspond with others

___Design   ___Invent

___Speak in public   ___Communicate verbally

___Remember information   ___Edit

___Write clearly   ___Think logically

___Research   ___Be ingenious

___Create new ideas

Leadership

___Arrange social functions   ___Direct others

___Motivate people   ___Exercise self-control

___Be competitive   ___Explain things to others

___Negotiate agreements   ___Motivate yourself

___Make decisions   ___Get results

___Plan   ___Solve problems

___Delegate   ___Mediate problems

___Run meetings   ___Take risks

Creative, Artistic

___Be artistic   ___Perform, act   ___Express yourself

___Appreciate music   ___Draw   ___Dance

___Present artistic   ___Play instruments
ideas

Other Transferable Skills You Have

Add any transferable skills that were not listed but that you think are important:

_____

_____

_____

_____

_____

Your Top Transferable Skills

Select the five top transferable skills you have that you want to use in your next job and list them below:

1. _____

2. _____

3. _____

4. _____

5. _____

The Skills Employers Want

To illustrate the importance of using your adaptive and transferable skills in your job, I have included the results of a survey of employers here. This information comes from a study of employers called "Workplace Basics—The Skills Employers Want." The study was conducted jointly by the U.S. Department of Labor and the American Association of Counseling and Development.

It turns out that most of the skills they want are either adaptive or transferable skills. Of course, specific job-related skills remain important, but basic skills form an essential foundation for success on the job. Here are the top skills employers identified:

1. Learning to learn
2. Basic academic skills in reading, writing, and computation
3. Good communication skills, including listening and speaking
4. Creative thinking and problem solving
5. Self-esteem, motivation, and goal setting
6. Personal and career development skills
7. Interpersonal/negotiation skills and teamwork
8. Organizational effectiveness and leadership

What is most interesting is that most of these skills are not formally taught in school. Of course, job-specific skills are also important (an accountant will still need to know accounting) but the adaptive and transferable skills are the ones that allow you to succeed in any job.

Again, this study shows the importance of being aware of your skills and using them well in career planning. If you have any weaknesses in one or more of the skills that were listed, consider improvements. And, always remember to turn your weaknesses into strengths. For example, if you don't have a specific skill that's required for a job, let the employer know that you don't but add that you are eager to learn and you are a quick study. This comment shows the employer that you are not afraid of learning new skills and that you are confident in your abilities. Furthermore, if you are already strong in one or more of the top skills employers want, look for opportunities to develop and use them in your work.

Identify Your Job-Related Skills

Many jobs require skills that are specific to that occupation. An airline pilot obviously needs to know how to fly an airplane; thankfully, having good adaptive and transferable skills would not be enough to be considered for that job.

Job-related skills may have been gained in a variety of ways, including education, training, work, hobbies, and other life experiences. As you complete the worksheets that follow, keep in mind that you are looking for skills and accomplishments. Pay special attention to those experiences that you really enjoyed. These experiences often demonstrate skills that you should try to use in your career choice.

When possible, quantify your activities or results with numbers to prove your accomplishments. Employers relate more easily to percentages, numbers, and ratios than to quality terms such as more, many, greater, less, fewer, and so on. For example, saying "presented to groups as large as 200 people" has more impact than "did many presentations."

EDUCATION AND TRAINING WORKSHEET

We spend many years in school and learn more lessons there than you might at first realize. For example, in our early years of schooling we acquire basic skills that are important in most jobs: getting along with others, reading instructions, and accepting supervision. Later on, courses become more specialized and relevant to potential careers.

This worksheet helps you review your education and training experiences, even those that may have occurred years ago. Some courses may seem more important to certain careers than others. But keep in mind that even the courses that don't seem to support a particular career choice can be an important source of skills.

Elementary School Experiences

While few employers will ask you about these years, jot down any highlights of things you felt particularly good about; doing so may help you identify important interests and directions to consider for the future. For example, note the following:

- Subjects you did well in that might relate to your ideal job

- Extracurricular activities/hobbies/leisure activities

- Accomplishments/things you did well (in or out of school)

(continued)

(continued)

High School Experiences

These experiences will be more important for a recent graduate and less so for those with college, work, or other life experiences. But, whatever your situation, what you did during these years can give you important clues to use in your career choice.

Name of school(s)/years attended:

_____

Subjects you did well in or might relate to your ideal career:

_____

_____

_____

Extracurricular activities/hobbies/leisure activities:

_____

_____

_____

Accomplishments/things you did well (in or out of school):

_____

_____

_____

_____

_____

Postsecondary Training or College Experiences

If you graduated from a two- or four-year college, took college classes, or attended other formal training or education programs after high school, what you learned and did during this time will be important for your career choice and of interest to employers. Emphasize here those things that you think directly support your ability to do a job.

Name of school(s)/years attended:

_____

_____

Major:

_____

Courses related to a job:

_____

_____

_____

_____

Extracurricular activities/hobbies/leisure activities:

_____

_____

_____

_____

Accomplishments/things you did well (in or out of school):

_____

_____

_____

_____

_____

Specific things you learned or can do that may relate to your career choice:

_____

_____

(continued)

(continued)

_____

_____

Additional Training and Education

There are many formal and informal ways to learn, and some of the most important things are often learned outside of the classroom. Use this worksheet to list any additional training or education that might relate to your career choice. Include military training, on-the-job training, workshops, or any other formal or informal training you have had. You can also include any substantial learning you obtained through a hobby, family activities, online research, or similar informal source.

Names of courses or programs/dates taken/any certificates or credentials earned:

_____

_____

_____

_____

_____

_____

Specific things you learned or can do that relate to the job you want:

_____

_____

_____

_____

_____

_____

THE JOB AND VOLUNTEER HISTORY WORKSHEET

Use this worksheet to list each major job you have held and the information related to each. Begin with your most recent job, followed by previous ones.

Include military experience and unpaid volunteer work here. Both are work and are particularly important if you do not have much paid civilian work experience. Create additional sheets to cover all of your significant jobs or unpaid experiences as needed. If you have been promoted, consider handling the new position as a separate job from the original position.

Whenever possible, provide numbers to support what you did: number of people served over one or more years; number of transactions processed; percent sales increase; total inventory value you were responsible for; payroll of the staff you supervised; total budget you were responsible for; and other specific data.

Job 1

Name of organization: _____

Address: _____

Job title(s): _____

Employed from: _____ to: _____

Computer, software, or other machinery or equipment you used:

_____

_____

_____

Data, information, or reports you created or used:

_____

_____

_____

(continued)

(continued)

People-oriented duties or responsibilities to coworkers, customers, others:

_____

_____

_____

_____

_____

Services you provided or products you produced:

_____

_____

_____

_____

_____

Reasons for promotions or salary increases, if any:

_____

_____

_____

_____

_____

Details on anything you did to help the organization, such as increase productivity, improve procedures or processes, simplify or reorganize job duties, decrease costs, increase profits, improve working conditions, reduce turnover, or other improvements. Quantify results when possible—for example, "Increased order processing by 50 percent, with no increase in staff costs."

_____

_____

Specific things you learned or can do that you would like to include in your ideal job:

_____

_____

_____

_____

_____

What would your supervisor say about you?

_____

_____

_____

_____

_____

Supervisor's name: _____

Phone number: _____ E-mail address: _____

Job 2

Name of organization: _____

Address: _____

Job title(s): _____

Employed from: _____ to: _____

Computer, software, or other machinery or equipment you used:

_____

_____

_____

Data, information, or reports you created or used:

_____

(continued)

(continued)

People-oriented duties or responsibilities to coworkers, customers, others:

Services you provided or products you produced:

Reasons for promotions or salary increases, if any:

Details on anything you did to help the organization, such as increase productivity, improve procedures or processes, simplify or reorganize job duties, decrease costs, increase profits, improve working conditions, reduce turnover, or other improvements. Quantify results when possible—for example, "Increased order processing by 50 percent, with no increase in staff costs."

_____

_____

Specific things you learned or can do that you would like to include in your ideal job:

_____

_____

_____

_____

What would your supervisor say about you?

_____

_____

_____

_____

Supervisor's name: _____

Phone number: _____ E-mail address: _____

Job 3

Name of organization: _____

Address: _____

Job title(s): _____

Employed from: _____ to: _____

Computer, software, or other machinery or equipment you used:

_____

_____

_____

(continued)

(continued)

Data, information, or reports you created or used:

_____

_____

_____

People-oriented duties or responsibilities to coworkers, customers, others:

_____

_____

_____

_____

_____

Services you provided or products you produced:

_____

_____

_____

_____

Reasons for promotions or salary increases, if any:

_____

_____

_____

_____

Details on anything you did to help the organization, such as increase productivity, improve procedures or processes, simplify or reorganize job duties, decrease costs, increase profits, improve working conditions, reduce turnover, or other improvements. Quantify results when possible—for example, "Increased order processing by 50 percent, with no increase in staff costs."

_____

_____

Specific things you learned or can do that you would like to include in your ideal job:

_____

_____

_____

_____

_____

What would your supervisor say about you?

_____

_____

_____

_____

_____

Supervisor's name: _____

Phone number: _____ E-mail address: _____

Job 4

Name of organization: _____

Address: _____

Job title(s): _____

Employed from: _____ to: _____

Computer, software, or other machinery or equipment you used:

_____

(continued)

(continued)

_____

_____

Data, information, or reports you created or used:

_____

_____

_____

People-oriented duties or responsibilities to coworkers, customers, others:

_____

_____

_____

_____

Services you provided or products you produced:

_____

_____

_____

_____

Reasons for promotions or salary increases, if any:

_____

_____

_____

_____

Details on anything you did to help the organization, such as increase productivity, improve procedures or processes, simplify or reorganize job duties, decrease costs, increase profits, improve working conditions, reduce turnover, or other improvements. Quantify results when possible—for example, "Increased order processing by 50 percent, with no increase in staff costs."

_____

_____

Specific things you learned or can do that you would like to include in your ideal job:

_____

_____

_____

_____

_____

What would your supervisor say about you?

_____

_____

_____

_____

_____

Supervisor's name: _____

Phone number: _____ E-mail address: _____

OTHER LIFE EXPERIENCES WORKSHEET

Many people overlook informal life experiences as being important sources of learning or accomplishment. This worksheet is here to encourage you to think about any hobbies or interests you have had—family responsibilities, recreational activities, travel, or any other experiences in your life where you feel some sense of accomplishment. Write any experiences that seem particularly meaningful to you, and name the key skills you think were involved.

Situation 1

Describe situation and skills used:

_____

_____

_____

_____

_____

Specific things you learned or can do that you would like to be part of your ideal job:

_____

_____

_____

_____

_____

Situation 2

Describe situation and skills used:

_____

_____

_____

_____

_____

Specific things you learned or can do that you would like to be part of your ideal job:

_____

_____

_____

_____

Situation 3

Describe situation and skills used:

_____

_____

_____

_____

Specific things you learned or can do that you would like to be part of your ideal job:

_____

_____

_____

_____

_____

Your Top Job-Related Skills

Of all the job-related skills you have, list the most important ones that you would like to include in your ideal career:

1. _____

2. _____

3. _____

(continued)

(continued)

4. _____

5. _____

Translate Your Knowledge of Your Skills to Your Career Choice

Knowing the skills you like to use can help you make a better decision about your future career. They are important for an employer to know about, but even more important for you to recognize.

Now that you have an awareness of your skill set, that information will become part of your career focus. Later, in Chapter 8, you will complete an "Overnight Career Choice Matrix" where you can list your best skills.

Key Points: Chapter 2

- Knowing what you are good at is an essential part of choosing a career. Unless you use the skills that you enjoy using and are good at, it is unlikely that you will be fully satisfied in your job.

- Adaptive skills, such as having good work habits and working well with others, are important to employers.

- Transferable skills, which include writing, managing people, and analyzing data, are useful in many careers.

- Job-related skills are those skills you have learned through education, training, and experience.

Chapter 3

What Interests You?

The second important step or factor in defining your ideal career is identifying your interests. The most effective system for connecting interests to careers was developed by the U.S. Department of Labor. Its research found that

- Your interests are an important source of information to use in exploring career options.

- You are more likely to be interested in things you are good at, you enjoy doing, or that are important to you.

- Your interests can accurately guide you to explore careers that are most likely to meet your needs.

Review 16 Career Interest Areas

Because exploring thousands of jobs is not practical, researchers organized all jobs into a small number of interest areas, which are explained in the following checklist. The interest areas are from the *New Guide for Occupational Exploration*, Fourth Edition, published by JIST Works. Originally developed as the *Guide for Occupational Exploration* by the Department of Labor, this system helps people explore career and learning options based on interests. The fourth edition updates the original *GOE*'s interest areas and other elements and aligns them with the U.S. Department of Education's 16 career clusters to closely link learning with careers.

You learn more about specific job titles in Chapter 6. For now, identify your top interests in the "Career Interest Areas Checklist" that follows.

CAREER INTEREST AREAS CHECKLIST

Read the definition of each interest area carefully. For each interest area, put a check mark by the option that best describes your interest in the interest area: "Not Interested," "Somewhat Interested or Not Sure," and "Very Interested."

1. Agriculture and Natural Resources. *An interest in working with plants, animals, forests, or mineral resources for agriculture, horticulture, conservation, extraction, and other purposes.* You can satisfy this interest by working in farming, landscaping, forestry, fishing, mining, and related fields. You may like doing physical work outdoors, such as on a farm or ranch, in a forest, or on a drilling rig. If you have scientific curiosity, you could study plants and animals or analyze biological or rock samples in a lab. If you have management ability, you could own, operate, or manage a fish hatchery, a landscaping business, or a greenhouse.

___Not Interested   ___Somewhat Interested or Not Sure
___Very Interested

2. Architecture and Construction. *An interest in designing, assembling, and maintaining components of buildings and other structures.* You may want to be part of the team of architects, drafters, and others who design buildings and render the plans. If construction interests you, you can find fulfillment in the many building projects that are being undertaken at all times. If you like to organize and plan, you can find careers in managing these projects. Or you can play a more direct role in putting up and finishing buildings by doing jobs such as plumbing, carpentry, masonry, painting, or roofing, either as a skilled craftsworker or as a helper. You can prepare the building site by operating heavy equipment or install, maintain, and repair vital building equipment and systems such as electricity and heating.

___Not Interested   ___Somewhat Interested or Not Sure
___Very Interested

3. Arts and Communication. *An interest in creatively expressing feelings or ideas, in communicating news or information, or in performing.* You can satisfy this interest in creative, verbal, or performing activities. For example, if you enjoy literature, perhaps writing or editing would appeal to you. Journalism and public relations are other fields for people who like to use their writing or speaking skills. Do you prefer to work in the performing arts? If so, you could direct or perform in drama, music, or dance. If you especially enjoy the visual arts, you could create paintings, sculpture, or ceramics or design products or visual displays. A flair for technology might lead you to specialize in photography, broadcast production, or dispatching.

___Not Interested   ___Somewhat Interested or Not Sure
___Very Interested

4. Business and Administration. *An interest in making a business organization or function run smoothly.* You can satisfy this interest by working in a position of leadership or by specializing in a function that contributes to the overall effort in a business, nonprofit organization, or government agency. If you especially enjoy working with people, you may find fulfillment from working in human resources. An interest in numbers may lead you to consider accounting, finance, budgeting, billing, or financial record-keeping. A job as an administrative assistant may interest you if you like a variety of work in a busy environment. If you are good with details and word processing, you may enjoy a job as a secretary or data entry keyer. Or perhaps you would do well as the manager of a business.

___Not Interested   ___Somewhat Interested or Not Sure
___Very Interested

5. Education and Training. *An interest in helping people learn. You can satisfy this interest by teaching students, who may be preschoolers, retirees, or any age in between.* You may specialize in a particular academic field or work with learners of a particular age, with a particular interest, or with a particular learning problem. Working in a library or museum may give you an opportunity to expand people's understanding of the world.

___Not Interested   ___Somewhat Interested or Not Sure
___Very Interested

6. Finance and Insurance. *An interest in helping businesses and people be assured of a financially secure future.* You can satisfy this interest by working in a financial or insurance business in a leadership or support role. If you like gathering and analyzing information, you may

(continued)

(continued)

find fulfillment as an insurance adjuster or financial analyst. Or you may deal with information at the clerical level as a banking or insurance clerk or in person-to-person situations providing customer service. Another way to interact with people is to sell financial or insurance services that will meet their needs.

___Not Interested   ___Somewhat Interested or Not Sure
___Very Interested

7. Government and Public Administration. *An interest in helping a government agency serve the needs of the public.* You can satisfy this interest by working in a position of leadership or by specializing in a function that contributes to the role of government. You may help protect the public by working as an inspector or examiner to enforce standards. If you enjoy using clerical skills, you may work as a clerk in a law court or government office. Or perhaps you prefer the top-down perspective of a government executive or urban planner.

___Not Interested   ___Somewhat Interested or Not Sure
___Very Interested

8. Health Science. *An interest in helping people and animals be healthy.* You can satisfy this interest by working in a health care team as a doctor, therapist, or nurse. You might specialize in one of the many different parts of the body (such as the teeth or eyes) or in one of the many different types of care. Or you may wish to be a generalist who deals with the whole patient. If you like technology, you might find satisfaction working with X rays or new methods of diagnosis. You might work with healthy people, helping them eat right. If you enjoy working with animals, you might care for them and keep them healthy.

___Not Interested   ___Somewhat Interested or Not Sure
___Very Interested

9. Hospitality, Tourism, and Recreation. *An interest in catering to the personal wishes and needs of others so that they may enjoy a clean environment, good food and drink, comfortable lodging away from home, and recreation.* You can satisfy this interest by providing services for the convenience, care, and pampering of others in hotels, restaurants, airplanes, beauty parlors, and so on. You may wish to use your love of cooking as a chef. If you like working with people, you may wish to provide personal services by being a travel guide, a flight attendant, a concierge, a hairdresser, or a waiter. You may wish to work in cleaning and building services if you like a clean environment. If you enjoy sports or games, you may work for an athletic team or casino.

___Not Interested   ___Somewhat Interested or Not Sure
___Very Interested

10. Human Service. *An interest in improving people's social, mental, emotional, or spiritual well-being.* You can satisfy this interest as a counselor, social worker, or religious worker who helps people sort out their complicated lives or solve personal problems. You may work as a caretaker for very young people or the elderly. Or you may interview people to help identify the social services they need.

___Not Interested   ___Somewhat Interested or Not Sure
___Very Interested

11. Information Technology. *An interest in designing, developing, managing, and supporting information systems.* You can satisfy this interest by working with hardware, software, multimedia, or integrated systems. If you like to use your organizational skills, you might work as an administrator of a system or database. Or you can solve complex problems as a software engineer or systems analyst. If you enjoy getting your hands on the hardware, you might find work servicing computers, peripherals, and information-intense machines such as cash registers and ATMs.

___Not Interested   ___Somewhat Interested or Not Sure
___Very Interested

12. Law and Public Safety. *An interest in upholding people's rights or in protecting people and property by using authority, inspecting, or investigating.* You can satisfy this interest by working in law, law enforcement, fire fighting, the military, and related fields. For example, if you enjoy mental challenge and intrigue, you could investigate crimes or fires for a living. If you enjoy working with verbal skills and research skills, you may want to defend citizens in court or research deeds, wills, and other legal documents. If you want to help people in critical situations, you may want to fight fires, work as a police

(continued)

(continued)

officer, or become a paramedic. Or, if you want more routine work in public safety, perhaps a job in guarding, patrolling, or inspecting would appeal to you. If you have management ability, you could seek a leadership position in law enforcement and the protective services. Work in the military gives you a chance to use technical and leadership skills while serving your country.

___Not Interested   ___Somewhat Interested or Not Sure
___Very Interested

13. Manufacturing. *An interest in processing materials into intermediate or final products or maintaining and repairing products by using machines or hand tools.* You can satisfy this interest by working in one of many industries that mass-produce goods or by working for a utility that distributes electric power or other resources. You may enjoy manual work, using your hands or hand tools in highly skilled jobs such as assembling engines or electronic equipment. If you enjoy making machines run efficiently or fixing them when they break down, you could seek a job installing or repairing such devices as copiers, aircraft engines, cars, or watches. Perhaps you prefer to set up or operate machines that are used to manufacture products made of food, glass, or paper. You may enjoy cutting and grinding metal and plastic parts to desired shapes and measurements. Or you may wish to operate equipment in systems that provide water and process wastewater. You may like inspecting, sorting, counting, or weighing products. Another option is to work with your hands and machinery to move boxes and freight in a warehouse. If leadership appeals to you, you could manage people engaged in production and repair.

___Not Interested   ___Somewhat Interested or Not Sure
___Very Interested

14. Retail and Wholesale Sales and Service. *An interest in bringing others to a particular point of view by personal persuasion and by sales and promotional techniques.* You can satisfy this interest in a variety of jobs that involve persuasion and selling. If you like using your knowledge of science, you may enjoy selling pharmaceutical, medical, or electronic products or services. Real estate offers several kinds of sales jobs as well. If you like speaking on the phone, you could work as a telemarketer. Or you may enjoy selling apparel and other merchandise in a retail setting. If you prefer to help people, you may want a job in customer service.

___Not Interested ___Somewhat Interested or Not Sure
___Very Interested

15. Scientific Research, Engineering, and Mathematics. *An interest in discovering, collecting, and analyzing information about the natural world; in applying scientific research findings to problems in medicine, the life sciences, human behavior, and the natural sciences; in imagining and manipulating quantitative data; and in applying technology to manufacturing, transportation, and other economic activities.* You can satisfy this interest by working with the knowledge and processes of the sciences. You may enjoy researching and developing new knowledge in mathematics, or perhaps solving problems in the physical, life, or social sciences would appeal to you. You may wish to study engineering and help create new machines, processes, and structures. If you want to work with scientific equipment and procedures, you could seek a job in a research or testing laboratory.

___Not Interested ___Somewhat Interested or Not Sure
___Very Interested

16. Transportation, Distribution, and Logistics. *An interest in operations that move people or materials.* You can satisfy this interest by managing a transportation service, by helping vehicles keep on their assigned schedules and routes, or by driving or piloting a vehicle. If you enjoy taking responsibility, perhaps managing a rail line would appeal to you. If you work well with details and can take pressure on the job, you might consider being an air traffic controller. Or would you rather get out on the highway, on the water, or up in the air? If so, then you could drive a truck from state to state, be employed on a ship, or fly a crop duster over a cornfield. If you prefer to stay closer to home, you could drive a delivery van, taxi, or school bus. You can use your physical strength to load freight and arrange it so it gets to its destination in one piece.

___Not Interested ___Somewhat Interested or Not Sure
___Very Interested

YOUR TOP INTEREST AREAS

Review each interest area from the previous table. Then write the three to five areas that interest you the most. Don't worry for now whether your choices are practical. Just list the interest areas that you would like to know more about, beginning with the area that interests you most.

1. _____

2. _____

3. _____

4. _____

5. _____

Look Closely at Career Clues for Your Top Interest Areas

Knowing your top interest areas gives you some idea of career areas to explore more carefully. The next worksheet helps you consider three important clues related to the career areas that interest you most. These clues are "Education and Training," "Work Experience," and "Leisure Activities." Your interests or activities in each of these areas can help you focus your career choice.

CAREER CLUES WORKSHEET

Look at the worksheet that follows. Where indicated, write your top interest areas from the "Your Top Interest Areas" box you just completed.

Now look at the next three columns of the worksheet. At the top of each column is one of the career clues. Use the blank space in each column to write notes related to each interest area you selected. Emphasize related activities you enjoyed or are good at. For example, people who select Agriculture and Natural Resources as a top interest area might write, in the "Education and Training Clues" column, that they liked and did well in biology and natural-science classes. In the "Work Experience Clues" column, they might write that they enjoyed a summer job working with horses at a riding stable. In the "Leisure Activities Clues" column, they might write that they like camping and hiking. Here are some ideas to help you decide what to write for each clue:

- **Education and Training.** Do you have education or training related to this interest? Include formal learning and school course names, and informal learning such as reading or on-the-job learning.

- **Work Experience.** Do you have work experience related to this interest? List any paid or unpaid work related to this interest. This can include full- and part-time jobs, volunteer work, work you do at home, and working in a family business.

- **Leisure Activities.** Do you have hobbies or leisure activities related to this interest? Anything you do that is not "work" gives you clues to your real interests. For example, think of magazines you read, clubs and organizations you belong to, extracurricular activities, hobbies, and other related leisure activities.

After you finish with your first interest area, do the same thing for the rest of your interest areas in the list. Instructions for filling in the empty circles come later.

CAREER PLANNING CLUES

Write Your Top Interest Areas Here	For each clue, write in things you enjoy doing or are good at that relate to each interest area.			Score
	Education and Training Clues	Work Experience Clues	Leisure Activities Clues	
1.	○	○	○	
2.	○	○	○	
3.	○	○	○	
4.	○	○	○	
5.	○	○	○	

Score Each Interest Area

After you have written your notes in each clue box, total your scores for each interest area. Begin with your first interest area. Under the "Education and Training Clues" column, decide which of the following statements best describes the activities you wrote in that clue box:

1. Activities do not strongly support this interest.

2. Activities provide some support for this interest.

3. Activities provide strong support for this interest.

Now notice the small circles in the lower-right corner of each clue box. This is where you should write the number of the statement you selected. Do this for each clue box for your first interest area. Do the same thing for each clue for the other interest areas. When you are done, add up the numbers you wrote in the three circles for each interest area and put that total in the "Score" column on the right.

What Your Scores Mean

Higher scores usually mean that you have spent more time on or are very interested in that interest area. You may have taken more related classes, spent more leisure time in related activities, or have more directly related work experience. Interest areas with your highest scores are the ones you should consider more closely. They are likely to offer careers that interest you most.

At this point, you have identified career clusters that interest you most and eliminated groups of careers that are not of interest. Chapter 6 helps you more clearly identify specific jobs within these interest areas to consider now or in the future.

Key Points: Chapter 3

- You are more likely to be interested in things you are good at, you enjoy doing, or that are important to you.

- The 16 career interest areas in the *New Guide for Occupational Exploration*, which is based on a system created by the U.S. Department of Labor, helps people explore career and learning options based on interests.

- Your education and training, past work experience, and leisure activities provide important clues to your top career interest areas.

Chapter 4

What Motivates and Is Important to You?

The third important consideration or step in your career choice is your personal values. What are your values? I once had a job where the sole reason for the existence of the organization was to make money. Not that this is necessarily wrong, it's just that I wanted to be involved in things that I could believe in. For example, some people work to help others, some to clean up our environment, and others to build things, make machines work, gain power or prestige, care for animals or plants, or something else.

Remember the surveys in Chapter 1 that showed most people want more than money from work? The checklist that follows helps you identify the values to include in your ideal career for the most satisfaction and success.

> **Tip:** *I believe that all work is worthwhile if done well, so the issue here is just what sorts of things motivate you and are important to you.*

Learn What You Value Most in a Career

This section presents 36 values that many people find important in their jobs.

✎ WORK VALUES CHECKLIST

Read each value and think about how important it is to you. Put a check mark in the column to the right of each value that best indicates how important that value is to include in your career.

Value	Not Important	Very Important	Important
1. **Help society:** Contribute to the betterment of the world I live in.			
2. **Help others:** Help others directly, either individually or in small groups.			
3. **Public contact:** Have lots of daily contact with people.			
4. **Teamwork/work with others:** Have close working relationships with a group; work as a team toward common goals.			
5. **Competition:** Compete against a goal or other people where there are clear outcomes.			
6. **Make decisions on my own:** Have the power to set policy and determine a course of action.			
7. **Have a pleasant work environment:** Be in a work environment I enjoy.			
8. **Be busy:** Have work that keeps me fully occupied and not bored.			
9. **Power and authority:** Have control over other people's work activities; be a manager or supervisor.			
10. **Influence people:** Be in a position to change other people's attitudes and opinions.			
11. **Work alone:** Do things by myself without much contact with or supervision by others.			
12. **Knowledge:** Seek knowledge, truth, and understanding.			
13. **Status:** Be looked up to by others at work and in the community or be recognized as a member of an organization whose work or status is important to me.			
14. **Artistic creativity:** Do creative work in writing, theater, art, design, or any other area.			

(continued)

(continued)

Value	Not Important	Very Important	Important
15. **General creativity:** Create new ideas, programs, or anything else that is new and different.			
16. **Teaching and instructing:** Have a job in which I teach or guide other people.			
17. **Change and variety:** Have job duties that often change or are done in different settings.			
18. **Free time:** Have work that allows me to have enough time for family, leisure, and other activities.			
19. **Quality:** Do work that allows me to meet high standards of excellence.			
20. **Stability:** Have job duties that are predictable and not likely to change over a long period of time.			
21. **Security:** Be fairly sure of keeping my job and not having to worry much about losing it.			
22. **Sense of accomplishment:** Have work that allows me to feel I am accomplishing something worthwhile or important.			
23. **Excitement:** Do work that is often exciting.			
24. **Adventure:** Do work that allows me to experience new things and take some risks.			
25. **Good coworkers:** Have a job where I like my coworkers and supervisor.			
26. **Earnings:** Be paid well compared to other workers.			
27. **Advancement:** Work that allows me to get training, experience, and opportunities to advance in pay and level of responsibility.			
28. **Independence:** Work for or by myself; decide for myself what kind of work I'll do and how I'll do it.			

Value	Not Important	Very Important	Important
29. **Location:** Have work that allows me to live in a town or geographic area that matches my lifestyle and allows me to do things I enjoy.			
30. **Physical challenge:** Have a job whose physical demands are challenging and rewarding.			
31. **Time freedom:** Have a flexible work schedule that allows me to have control of my time.			
32. **Beauty:** Have a job that allows me to enjoy or that involves sensitivity to or for beauty.			
33. **Friendship:** Have work that develops close personal relationships with coworkers.			
34. **Recognition:** Be recognized for the quality of my work in some visible or public way.			
35. **Moral fulfillment:** Feel that my work is contributing to a set of moral standards that I feel are very important.			
36. **Community:** Live in a town or city where I can get involved in community affairs.			

Other Values or Preferences: Write other work values or preferences that are very important to you and that you want to include in your career planning.

_____

_____

_____

_____

_____

Rank Your Most Important Values

Next, use the following worksheet to rank the top values that you would like to include in your ideal career.

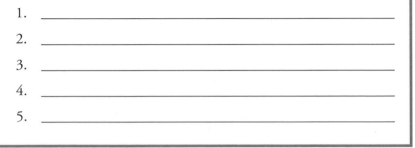

YOUR MOST IMPORTANT VALUES

Look over the checklist you just completed. Select the five values you would *most* like to include in your career or job and list them below. List them in order of importance to you, beginning with the most important value. These are the values you should consider most when selecting a career or making other important life decisions.

1. _____

2. _____

3. _____

4. _____

5. _____

Key Points: Chapter 4

- Including your personal values in your ideal career will give you the most satisfaction and success.

- Work values include creativity, stability, independence, good coworkers, a sense of accomplishment, advancement, excitement, change and variety, helping others, and recognition.

- Keep your top values in mind when making your career choice and other important life decisions.

Chapter 5

Other Key Considerations When Defining Your Ideal Job

Earlier chapters focused on the first three key considerations for defining your ideal job: your skills and abilities, your interests, and your personal values.

This chapter covers the six other important factors or steps:

- Preferred earnings
- Level of responsibility
- Location
- Special knowledge
- Work environment
- Types of people you like to work with and for

Keeping these points in mind will help you pinpoint a career that will make you successful in many ways.

How Much Money Do You Want to Make—or Are You Willing to Accept?

As you read in Chapter 1, research shows that pay is not the most important thing for most people. Even so, many people use pay rates as a primary reason for selecting one career over another.

It's easy to say that money isn't important, but it is. Earnings are particularly important for those starting out and for those with lower incomes. How much you earn is also an issue for most working people.

While money may not be everything, when deciding your career focus, it is important to consider the money issue in advance. Doing so now will help you make a good decision later, when you receive a job offer, and have to balance the money with other factors. For example, would you take a position ideal for you in many ways if the money was a bit less than you wanted?

The Price of Happiness

I remember a middle-aged executive who had made over $80,000 per year. He had been unemployed for some time and was quite depressed. When asked what he wanted to earn in his next job, he told me that he wanted to start at about $85,000 but that he really only needed $40,000 per year to maintain his lifestyle now that his kids were grown. He also told me that he and his spouse liked where they lived, did not want to leave, and would settle for less money if they could stay where they were.

I suggested he redefine his job objective to include jobs he would enjoy doing and not to screen out jobs paying less than $80,000 per year. With a more flexible approach, he quickly accepted a job paying $47,000 and loved it. He told me he would never consider going back to what he did before, whatever the salary.

YOUR ACCEPTABLE PAY RANGE

Pay is important, but relative. What you want to earn in your next job and in the future affects your career choice. You need to consider that some compromise on money is always possible. This is why you should know in advance the pay you would accept, in addition to what you would prefer. Here are a few questions to help you define your salary range:

1. If you found the perfect job in all other respects, what would be the very least pay you would be willing to accept (per hour, week, or year)?

    _____

2. What is the upper end of pay you could expect to obtain, given your credentials and other factors?

    _____

3. What sort of income would you need to pay for a desirable lifestyle? (However you want to define this.)

    _____

4. How much money do you hope to make in your next job?

_____

Many people will take less money if the job is great in other ways—
or if they simply need to survive. And we all want more pay if we can
get it. Realistically, your next job will probably be somewhere
between your minimum and maximum amount. Complete the following to determine a reasonable pay range for your next position.

Reasonable lower end of what you will accept on your next position

_____

Reasonable upper end of pay you can expect on your next job

_____

How Much Responsibility Are You Willing to Accept?

In most organizations, those who are willing to accept more responsibility
are also typically paid more. With few exceptions, if you want to earn
more, you will have to accept more responsibility or get more education.
Higher levels of responsibility often require you to supervise others or
make decisions that affect the organization. When things don't go well,
people in charge are held accountable for the performance of their area of
responsibility. Some people are willing to accept this responsibility and
others, understandably, would prefer not to. Decide how much responsibility you are willing to accept and write that in the next worksheet.

YOUR PREFERRED LEVEL OF RESPONSIBILITY

Here are some questions to help you consider how much responsibility
you want or are willing to accept in your ideal job.

1. Do you like to be in charge? _____

2. Are you good at supervising others? _____

(continued)

(continued)

3. Do you prefer working as part of a team? _____

4. Do you prefer working by yourself or under someone else's guidance? _____

Jot down where you see yourself, in terms of accepting responsibility for others, and in other ways within an organization.

_____

_____

_____

_____

Where Do You Want Your Ideal Job to Be Located—in What City or Region?

One factor to consider when choosing a career is where, geographically, you want to work. This could be as simple a decision as finding a job that allows you to live where you are now. This might be because you want to live near your relatives, like where you live and don't want to move, or want to be close to your favorite childcare center. Maybe you are or are not willing to relocate across town or to a distant city.

There are often good reasons for wanting to stay where you now live, although certain career opportunities may be limited unless you are willing to move. For example, if you live in a small town, some jobs may exist in small numbers, if at all. If you are willing to leave, you may be able to find jobs with higher overall wages, a larger and more varied job market, or some other advantage.

Tip: *If you decide to stay where you are, there are still geographic issues to consider. How far are you, for example, willing to commute? Do you want or need to take public transportation? Would it be more desirable for you to work on one side of town than the other?*

When you've looked at all the options, you can make a more informed decision. If you prefer to stay but are willing to move, a good strategy is to spend a substantial part of your job search time looking locally. If you are willing to relocate, don't make the common mistake of looking for a job "anywhere." That sort of scattered approach is both inefficient and ineffective. It is preferable to narrow your job search to a few key geographic areas and concentrate your efforts there.

Keep in mind that the right job in the wrong place is not the right job. A better course of action is to define the characteristics of the place you'd like to live.

For example, suppose you would like to live near the mountains, in a mid-sized city, and in a part of the country that has mild winters but does have four seasons. That leaves out a large number of places, doesn't it? Or it may be as simple as wanting to live near your mom. As you add more criteria, there are fewer and fewer places to look, and your job search becomes more precise. The more precise you are, the more likely you will end up with what you want. One way to do this is to consider the places you have already lived. Think about what you did and did not like about them. Use a sheet of paper to list the things you did like (on the left side) and did not like (on the right). This may help you identify the things you would like to have in a new place. You should also go to your library or the Internet to research a particular location you are considering or just to learn about the options.

PREFERRED GEOGRAPHIC LOCATION

Go ahead and write down where you prefer your work to be located.

_____

_____

_____

_____

_____

_____

What Special Knowledge or Interests Would You Like to Use or Pursue?

You have all sorts of life experiences, training, and education that can help you succeed in a new career. Chapter 2 helped you to record this information in detail, and you might want to look over that material before responding to the questions in this section.

Perhaps you know how to fix computers, write well, build things, keep accounting records, solve problems, or cook good food. Write down the things you have learned from schooling, training, hobbies, family experiences, and other formal or informal sources. Perhaps one or more of them could make you a very special applicant in the right setting. For example, an accountant who knows a lot about fashion would be a very special candidate if he or she wants a career with an organization that sells clothing, home furnishings, or has another connection to style and fashion.

Formal education, special training, and work experience are obviously important, but leisure activities, hobbies, volunteer work, family responsibilities, and other informal activities can also help define a previously overlooked job possibility.

To help you consider alternatives, use a separate sheet of paper to make a list of the major areas in which you

1. Have received formal education or training

2. Have learned to do something from prior on-the-job, hobby, or other informal experience

3. Are very interested in, but don't have much practical experience

Once you have made your list, go back and select the areas that are most interesting to you. These could give you ideas for jobs you might otherwise overlook. List your top special knowledge or interest choices on the worksheet that follows, beginning with the one that is most important to you.

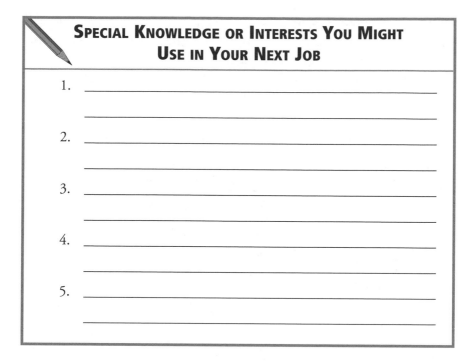

SPECIAL KNOWLEDGE OR INTERESTS YOU MIGHT USE IN YOUR NEXT JOB

1. _____

2. _____

3. _____

4. _____

5. _____

As you fine-tune your career choice, try to include at least one or two of your special interests or knowledge. For instance, if you are looking for a job as a warehouse manager but selected your hobby of making pottery as an area where you have special knowledge, can you think of a possible job combining the two? Perhaps distributing pottery supplies or managing some part of a pottery business would be more your cup of tea than just managing any sort of warehouse.

What Sort of Work Environment Do You Prefer?

I don't like to work in a building without windows, and I do like to get up and move around occasionally. While most of us can put up with all sorts of less-than-ideal work environments, some work environment issues will bother you more than others.

Once again, defining the things you did not like about previous work and school environments is a good way to help you define what you prefer. Think of all the places you've worked or gone to school and write down the things you didn't like about those environments. Then redefine them as positives, as in the following example. When you have completed the list for each job you've had (use extra sheets if necessary), go back and select the five environmental preferences that are really important to you. Here is one example of such a worksheet to help you get started.

Job: Accountant for the Internal Revenue Service

Things I Did Not Like About the Workplace	Environment I Would Like in My Next Job
too noisy	quiet workplace
no variety in work	lots of variety in work
no windows	my own window
parking was a problem	my own air strip (just kidding)
too much sitting	more activity
not people-oriented	more customer contact
indoors in nice weather	more outside work
too large an organization	smaller organization

Other issues to consider when defining your ideal work environment include frequent travel, work hazards, job stress, and physical demands.

YOUR PREFERRED WORK ENVIRONMENT

Write down those things about your work environment that are most important to include in your next job on the lines below. List your most important selection first, followed by others in order of importance.

1. _____

_____

2. _____

_____

3. _____

_____

4. _____

_____

5. _____

_____

What Types of People Do You Prefer to Work With?

An important element in enjoying your job is the people you work with and for. If you have ever had a rotten boss or worked with a group of losers, you know exactly why this is so important. Keep in mind that what someone else defines as a good group of people to work with might not be good for you.

You could argue that there is no way to know in advance the types of people you will end up having as coworkers. However, first impressions work both ways. Your potential employer judges you within the first 30 seconds of a face-to-face meeting. You can do the same regarding your potential boss and coworkers. This is why it is a good idea to meet with the people you will work with before you accept a position. Ask them questions if you can't get a good read on the type of people they are. If you haven't already given any thought to the subject, the following exercise will help you do just that.

Think about all your past jobs (work, military, volunteer, school, and so on) and your coworkers on those jobs. Write down the things you didn't like about your coworkers, and then redefine them into qualities you'd like to see in your work mates. When your list is complete, go back and identify the types of people you would really like to work with in your next job. Then select the five qualities that are most important to you.

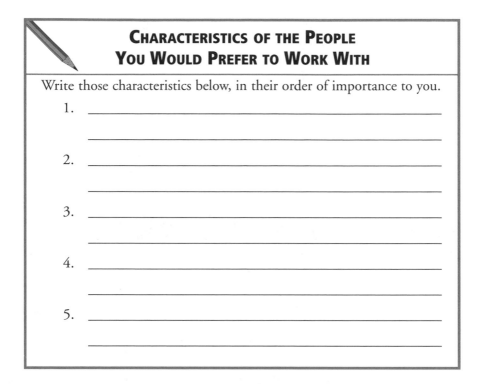

**CHARACTERISTICS OF THE PEOPLE
YOU WOULD PREFER TO WORK WITH**

Write those characteristics below, in their order of importance to you.

1. _____

_____

2. _____

_____

3. _____

_____

4. _____

_____

5. _____

_____

You Have Defined Nine Ideal Career Characteristics

The activities you completed in Chapters 1 through 5 have helped you more clearly define the preferred characteristics of your next career—and we haven't reviewed job titles or industries yet! Any one of these preferred characteristics, if left unresolved, can cause you problems during your search for a job. Even worse, pursuing a career that is in major conflict with one or more of these factors can lead to job failure or unhappiness.

So spend whatever time is needed to resolve each of the nine factors so that you are clear what you would prefer in your ideal job.

Key Points: Chapter 5

- While money may not be everything, when deciding your career focus, it is important to consider the money issue in advance so you can make good choices.

- Decide how much responsibility you are willing to accept in your career.

- Keep in mind that the right job in the wrong place is not the right job. A better course of action is to define the characteristics of the place you'd like to live.

- You have all sorts of life experience, training, and education that can help you succeed in a new career. Include the experiences you enjoy the most in your definition of your ideal career.

- Your work environment plays a role in your contentment on the job.

- An important element in enjoying your job is the people you work with and for. If you have ever had a rotten boss or worked with a group of losers, you know exactly why this is so important.

Chapter 6

Finally! Identify
Specific Job Titles

B y now you should have a better sense of
your skills, interests, work values, and
other key elements of your ideal career. Keep
those factors in mind as you review the job
descriptions in this chapter.

This chapter is designed to give you a good
idea of what sort of job you want in terms of
a job title. It is the longest chapter in the
book and describes more than 275 major job
titles, including their education or training
required, skill levels, earnings, growth, and
other details to help you make a good decision. Although this chapter is long, don't
worry. You won't need to read it all.

> **Note:** *You may have
> expected this chapter at
> the beginning of the
> book. I have not pre-
> sented job titles until
> now because I want to
> shake you out of the
> conventional approach
> that focuses narrowly on
> job titles. That narrow
> focus causes people to
> overlook far more
> important matters for
> their long-term career
> satisfaction and success.*

Why Accurate Information About
Specific Jobs Is Important

You have identified your interests and learned about other factors to consider in your career choice. But how can you identify specific jobs that
would be best for you? Will they require more training or education? What
do they pay? Do they offer good opportunity?

Accurate information about specific jobs is important for your career planning, but you have thousands of job titles to consider. Even within one
interest area, there are many jobs at different levels of pay, with different
levels of required training, and with very different work settings.

For example, in the health field you might consider being a medical doctor,
an emergency medical technician, or a home health-care worker. Each of
these jobs has very different entry requirements, pay, and tasks. These

differences affect your education, workday, work environment, pay, lifestyle, and more. That's why accurate job descriptions can help you make good career decisions.

The jobs described in this chapter appear in a longer form in the *Occupational Outlook Handbook,* a book published every two years by the U.S. Department of Labor and available from JIST. The *OOH* is also available online at www.careeroink.com and at http://www.bls.gov/oco/home.htm. The data in the job descriptions comes from research done by the U.S. Department of Labor.

How the Job Descriptions Are Organized

Although there are many career options to consider, the following information makes the task easier. In Chapter 3, you reviewed 16 career interest areas and identified those that interested you most.

This chapter organizes job descriptions into those same 16 interest areas. Within each interest area are the names of "work groups" of similar or related jobs. Following each work group are specific job descriptions related to it. The interest areas and work groups are taken from the *New Guide for Occupational Exploration,* Fourth Edition, which is published by JIST.

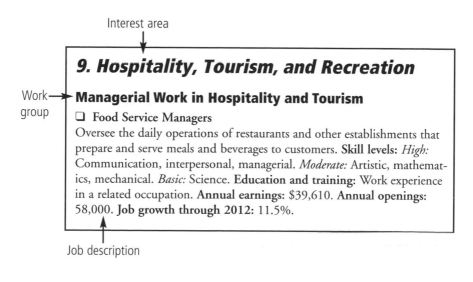

Interest area

9. Hospitality, Tourism, and Recreation

Work group

Managerial Work in Hospitality and Tourism

❑ **Food Service Managers**
Oversee the daily operations of restaurants and other establishments that prepare and serve meals and beverages to customers. **Skill levels:** *High:* Communication, interpersonal, managerial. *Moderate:* Artistic, mathematics, mechanical. *Basic:* Science. **Education and training:** Work experience in a related occupation. **Annual earnings:** $39,610. **Annual openings:** 58,000. **Job growth through 2012:** 11.5%.

Job description

Review Job Titles

Refer to Chapter 3 to recall your top interest areas. Then highlight or circle your top interest areas in the pages that follow.

Then skim the job titles listed under your top interest areas. Checkmark the jobs that sound most interesting to you. When you checkmark a job, also look closely at the related jobs in its work group to identify other possible job options. Continue with your other top interest areas and checkmark all the related jobs that interest you. Some jobs are listed more than once because they fit into more than one interest area or work group.

The job descriptions are pretty easy to understand. They begin with the formal job title, followed by a brief description of the job. The skill levels required for the job are listed. The skill information is followed by the level of education or training typically needed for entry to the job, annual earnings for those working in the job, projected number of job openings per year, and projected job growth through 2012. Note that earnings are "median" earnings, where half of all workers in that job earn less and half more. New or less-experienced workers typically earn less. Additional information on the job descriptions appears at the end of the chapter.

> **Note:** *Don't read each job description at this time. Just check the ones that interest you. Checkmark jobs that interest you even if you don't have the education for that job or if there is some other barrier. Later, you will be asked to read your checked jobs more carefully and select those that most interest you. For now, simply check the jobs that are even somewhat interesting to you.*

1. Agriculture and Natural Resources

Managerial Work in Agriculture and Natural Resources

❑ **Conservation Scientists and Foresters**
Manage, improve, and protect forested lands and other natural resources to maximize their use without damaging the environment. **Skill levels:** *High:* Mathematics, mechanical, science. *Moderate:* Communication, managerial. *Basic:* Interpersonal. *Not essential:* Artistic. **Education and training:** Bachelor's degree. **Annual earnings:** $50,677. **Annual openings:** 2,000. **Job growth through 2012:** 4.4%.

❑ **Farmers, Ranchers, and Agricultural Managers**

On an ownership or rental basis, operate farms, ranches, greenhouses, nurseries, timber tracts, or other agricultural production establishments that produce crops, horticultural specialties, livestock, poultry, finfish, shellfish, or animal specialties. **Skill levels:** *High:* Communication, interpersonal, managerial, mechanical. *Moderate:* Mathematics, science. *Not essential:* Artistic. **Education and training:** Long-term on-the-job training. **Annual earnings:** $42,065. **Annual openings:** 143,000. **Job growth through 2012:** –16.5%.

❑ **Purchasing Managers, Buyers, and Purchasing Agents**

Seek to obtain the highest-quality merchandise at the lowest possible purchase cost for employers. Buy goods and services for use by a company or organization, or buy items for resale. **Skill levels:** *High:* Communication, interpersonal, managerial. *Moderate:* Mathematics. *Basic:* Science. *Not essential:* Artistic, mechanical. **Education and training:** Work experience in a related occupation. **Annual earnings:** $51,010. **Annual openings:** 64,000. **Job growth through 2012:** 7.8%.

Resource Science/Engineering for Plants, Animals, and the Environment

❑ **Agricultural and Food Scientists**

Conduct research in the genetics, production, growth, and yield of farm animals and crops; develop ways of improving their quantity and quality; or study the principles underlying the nutritional value of foods. **Skill levels:** *High:* Mathematics, mechanical, science. *Moderate:* Communication, managerial. *Basic:* Interpersonal. *Not essential:* Artistic. **Education and training:** Bachelor's degree. **Annual earnings:** $50,952. **Annual openings:** 2,000. **Job growth through 2012:** 9.1%.

❑ **Agricultural Engineers**

Apply knowledge of engineering technology and biological science to agriculture; design agricultural machinery and equipment and agricultural structures. **Skill levels:** *High:* Mathematics, mechanical, science. *Moderate:* Communication, managerial. *Basic:* Artistic, interpersonal. **Education and training:** Bachelor's degree. **Annual earnings:** $56,520. **Annual openings:** fewer than 500. **Job growth through 2012:** 10.3%.

❑ **Biological Scientists**

Study living organisms and their relationship to their environment; research problems dealing with life processes; usually specialize in some area of biology, such as zoology (the study of animals) or microbiology (the study of microscopic organisms). **Skill levels:** *High:* Mathematics, mechanical, science. *Moderate:* Communication, managerial. *Basic:* Interpersonal. *Not essential:* Artistic. **Education and training:** Doctoral degree. **Annual earnings:** $58,428. **Annual openings:** 4,000. **Job growth through 2012:** 17.2%.

❑ **Conservation Scientists and Foresters**
Manage, improve, and protect forested lands and other natural resources to maximize their use without damaging the environment. **Skill levels:** *High:* Mathematics, mechanical, science. *Moderate:* Communication, managerial. *Basic:* Interpersonal. *Not essential:* Artistic. **Education and training:** Bachelor's degree. **Annual earnings:** $50,677. **Annual openings:** 2,000. **Job growth through 2012:** 4.4%.

❑ **Environmental Engineers**
Use the principles of biology and chemistry to develop solutions to environmental problems, such as water and air pollution control, recycling, waste disposal, and public health issues. **Skill levels:** *High:* Mathematics, mechanical, science. *Moderate:* Communication, managerial. *Basic:* Artistic, interpersonal. **Education and training:** Bachelor's degree. **Annual earnings:** $66,480. **Annual openings:** 6,000. **Job growth through 2012:** 38.2%.

❑ **Mining and Geological Engineers, Including Mine Safety Engineers**
Determine the location and plan the extraction of coal, metallic ores, nonmetallic minerals, and building materials, such as stone and gravel. **Skill levels:** *High:* Mathematics, mechanical, science. *Moderate:* Communication, managerial. *Basic:* Artistic, interpersonal. **Education and training:** Bachelor's degree. **Annual earnings:** $64,690. **Annual openings:** Fewer than 500. **Job growth through 2012:** –2.7%.

❑ **Petroleum Engineers**
Devise methods to improve oil and gas well production and determine the need for new or modified tool designs. Oversee drilling and offer technical advice to achieve economical and satisfactory progress. **Skill levels:** *High:* Mathematics, mechanical, science. *Moderate:* Communication, managerial. *Basic:* Artistic, interpersonal. **Education and training:** Bachelor's degree. **Annual earnings:** $88,500. **Annual openings:** 1,000. **Job growth through 2012:** –9.8%.

General Farming

❑ **Agricultural Workers**

Plant and harvest crops, install irrigation, deliver animals, and make sure that food is safe. **Skill levels:** *High:* Mechanical. *Basic:* Communication, interpersonal, managerial, mathematics, science. *Not essential:* Artistic. **Education and training:** Moderate-term on-the-job training. **Annual earnings:** $18,676. **Annual openings:** 40,000. **Job growth through 2012:** 6.2%.

Nursery, Groundskeeping, and Pest Control

❑ **Grounds Maintenance Workers**

Perform tasks necessary to achieve a pleasant and functional outdoor environment, or to care for indoor gardens and plantings in commercial and public facilities, such as malls, hotels, and botanical gardens. **Skill levels:** *High:* Mechanical. *Moderate:* Artistic. *Basic:* Communication, mathematics, science. *Not essential:* Interpersonal, managerial. **Education and training:** Short-term on-the-job training. **Annual earnings:** $20,832. **Annual openings:** 24,987. **Job growth through 2012:** 21.5%.

❑ **Pest Control Workers**

Spray or release chemical solutions or toxic gases and set traps to kill pests and vermin, such as mice, termites, and roaches, that infest buildings and surrounding areas. **Skill levels:** *High:* Mechanical. *Basic:* Communication, mathematics, science. *Not essential:* Artistic, interpersonal, managerial. **Education and training:** Moderate-term on-the-job training. **Annual earnings:** $26,220. **Annual openings:** 11,000. **Job growth through 2012:** 17.0%.

Forestry and Logging

❑ **Forestry, Conservation, and Logging Workers**

Help develop, maintain, and protect the forests by growing and planting new seedlings, fighting insects and diseases that attack trees, and helping to control soil erosion; or harvest trees on a tree farm or in a forest. **Skill levels:** *High:* Mechanical. *Basic:* Communication, interpersonal, managerial, mathematics, science. *Not essential:* Artistic. **Education and training:** Moderate-term on-the-job training. **Annual earnings:** $25,884. **Annual openings:** 17,000. **Job growth through 2012:** 1.9%.

Hunting and Fishing

❑ **Fishers and Fishing Vessel Operators**

Use nets, fishing rods, traps, or other equipment to catch and gather fish or other aquatic animals from rivers, lakes, or oceans for human consumption or other uses. May haul game onto ship or work on a fish farm. **Skill levels:** *High:* Mechanical. *Moderate:* Communication. *Basic:* Interpersonal, managerial, mathematics, science. *Not essential:* Artistic. **Education and training:** Moderate-term on-the-job training. **Annual earnings:** $24,100. **Annual openings:** 6,000. **Job growth through 2012:** –26.8%.

Mining and Drilling

❑ **Material Moving Occupations**

Use machinery to move construction materials, earth, petroleum products, and other heavy materials, generally over short distances; manually handle freight, stock, or other materials; clean equipment; or feed materials into processing machinery. **Skill levels:** *High:* Mechanical. *Basic:* Communication. *Not essential:* Artistic, interpersonal, managerial, mathematics, science. **Education and training:** Moderate-term on-the-job training. **Annual earnings:** $26,896. **Annual openings:** 930,000. **Job growth through 2012:** –1.5%.

2. Architecture and Construction

Managerial Work in Architecture and Construction

❑ **Construction Managers**

Plan, direct, coordinate, or budget, usually through subordinate supervisory personnel, activities concerned with the construction and maintenance of structures, facilities, and systems. **Skill levels:** *High:* Communication, interpersonal, managerial, mathematics, mechanical. *Moderate:* Science. *Basic:* Artistic. **Education and training:** Bachelor's degree. **Annual earnings:** $69,870. **Annual openings:** 47,000. **Job growth through 2012:** 12.0%.

Architectural Design

❑ **Architects, Except Landscape and Marine**

Plan and design structures, such as private residences, office buildings, theaters, factories, and other structural property. **Skill levels:** *High:* Artistic, mathematics, mechanical. *Moderate:* Communication, interpersonal, managerial, science. **Education and training:** Bachelor's degree. **Annual earnings:** $60,300. **Annual openings:** 8,000. **Job growth through 2012:** 17.3%.

❑ **Landscape Architects**

Plan and design land areas for such projects as parks and other recreational facilities, airports, highways, hospitals, schools, land subdivisions, and commercial, industrial, and residential sites. **Skill levels:** *High:* Artistic, mechanical. *Moderate:* Communication, interpersonal, managerial, mathematics, science. **Education and training:** Bachelor's degree. **Annual earnings:** $53,120. **Annual openings:** 2,000. **Job growth through 2012:** 22.2%.

Architecture/Construction Engineering Technologies

❑ **Construction and Building Inspectors**

Inspect structures using engineering skills to determine structural soundness and compliance with specifications, building codes, and other regulations. **Skill levels:** *High:* Mechanical. *Moderate:* Science. *Basic:* Communication, interpersonal, managerial, mathematics. *Not essential:* Artistic. **Education and training:** Work experience in a related occupation. **Annual earnings:** $43,670. **Annual openings:** 10,000. **Job growth through 2012:** 13.8%.

❑ **Drafters**

Prepare technical drawings and plans to serve as visual guidelines for production and construction workers, show the technical details of products and structures, and specify dimensions, materials, and procedures. **Skill levels:** *High:* Artistic, mechanical. *Moderate:* Communication, mathematics. *Basic:* Interpersonal, science. *Not essential:* Managerial. **Education and training:** Postsecondary vocational award. **Annual earnings:** $41,162. **Annual openings:** 28,000. **Job growth through 2012:** 2.8%.

❑ **Surveyors, Cartographers, Photogrammetrists, and Surveying Technicians**

Measure and map earth's surface. May establish official land, air space, and water boundaries; provide data relevant to the shape, contour, location, elevation, or dimension of land features; or compile geographic, political, and cultural information. **Skill levels:** *Moderate:* Artistic, communication, interpersonal, mathematics, mechanical, science. *Basic:* Managerial. **Education and training:** Bachelor's degree. **Annual earnings:** $37,155. **Annual openings:** 17,000. **Job growth through 2012:** 14.1%.

Construction Crafts

❏ **Boilermakers**

Construct, assemble, maintain, and repair stationary steam boilers and boiler house auxiliaries. Align structures or plate sections to assemble boiler frame tanks or vats following blueprints. **Skill levels:** *High:* Mechanical. *Basic:* Artistic, communication, interpersonal, mathematics, science. *Not essential:* Managerial. **Education and training:** Long-term on-the-job training. **Annual earnings:** $45,100. **Annual openings:** 2,000. **Job growth through 2012:** 1.7%.

❏ **Bricklayers, Blockmasons, and Stonemasons**

Lay and bind building materials, such as brick, structural tile, concrete block, cinder block, glass block, terra-cotta block, and stone, with mortar and other substances to construct or repair walls, partitions, arches, sewers, and other structures. **Skill levels:** *High:* Mechanical. *Moderate:* Artistic. *Basic:* Communication, interpersonal, mathematics, science. *Not essential:* Managerial. **Education and training:** Long-term on-the-job training. **Annual earnings:** $41,044. **Annual openings:** 23,000. **Job growth through 2012:** 14.2%.

❏ **Carpenters**

Construct, erect, install, or repair structures and fixtures made of wood, such as concrete forms; building frameworks, including partitions, joists, studding, and rafters; wood stairways; window and door frames; and hardwood floors. **Skill levels:** *High:* Mechanical. *Moderate:* Artistic, mathematics. *Basic:* Communication, interpersonal, science. *Not essential:* Managerial. **Education and training:** Long-term on-the-job training. **Annual earnings:** $34,900. **Annual openings:** 193,000. **Job growth through 2012:** 10.1%.

❏ **Carpet, Floor, and Tile Installers and Finishers**

Apply blocks, tiles, strips, or sheets of shock-absorbing, sound-deadening, or decorative coverings to floors and decks. May scrape and sand wooden floors to smooth surfaces and apply coats of finish. **Skill levels:** *High:* Mechanical. *Moderate:* Artistic. *Basic:* Communication, interpersonal, mathematics, science. *Not essential:* Managerial. **Education and training:** Moderate-term on-the-job training. **Annual earnings:** $33,313. **Annual openings:** 20,000. **Job growth through 2012:** 16.8%.

❏ **Cement Masons, Concrete Finishers, Segmental Pavers, and Terrazzo Workers**
Place and finish concrete walls, sidewalks, beams, columns, and panels; lay out, cut, and install flat pieces of masonry to pave paths, patios, playgrounds, driveways, and steps; or apply a mixture of cement, sand, pigment, or marble chips to surfaces. **Skill levels:** *High:* Mechanical. *Moderate:* Artistic. *Basic:* Communication, interpersonal, mathematics, science. *Not essential:* Managerial. **Education and training:** Moderate-term on-the-job training. **Annual earnings:** $31,291. **Annual openings:** 25,000. **Job growth through 2012:** 25.8%.

❏ **Construction Equipment Operators**
Use machinery to move construction materials, earth, and other heavy materials and to apply asphalt and concrete to roads and other structures. **Skill levels:** *High:* Mechanical. *Basic:* Communication, interpersonal, mathematics, science. *Not essential:* Artistic, managerial. **Education and training:** Moderate-term on-the-job training. **Annual earnings:** $34,719. **Annual openings:** 54,000. **Job growth through 2012:** 10.7%.

❏ **Drywall Installers, Ceiling Tile Installers, and Tapers**
Apply plasterboard or other wallboard to ceilings or interior walls of buildings, apply or mount acoustical tiles or shock-absorbing materials to ceilings and walls of buildings to reduce or reflect sound, or seal joints between panels. **Skill levels:** *High:* Mechanical. *Basic:* Artistic, communication, interpersonal, mathematics, science. *Not essential:* Managerial. **Education and training:** Moderate-term on-the-job training. **Annual earnings:** $35,204. **Annual openings:** 22,000. **Job growth through 2012:** 21.3%.

❏ **Electricians**
Install, maintain, and repair electrical wiring, equipment, and fixtures. Ensure that work is in accordance with relevant codes. May install or service street lights, intercom systems, or electrical control systems. **Skill levels:** *High:* Mechanical. *Moderate:* Mathematics, science. *Basic:* Communication, interpersonal. *Not essential:* Artistic, managerial. **Education and training:** Long-term on-the-job training. **Annual earnings:** $42,300. **Annual openings:** 65,000. **Job growth through 2012:** 23.4%.

❏ **Glaziers**
Install glass in windows, skylights, store fronts, and display cases, or on surfaces, such as building fronts, interior walls, ceilings, and tabletops. **Skill**

levels: *High:* Mechanical. *Moderate:* Artistic. *Basic:* Communication, interpersonal, mathematics, science. *Not essential:* Managerial. **Education and training:** Long-term on-the-job training. **Annual earnings:** $32,650. **Annual openings:** 7,000. **Job growth through 2012:** 17.2%.

❑ **Hazardous Materials Removal Workers**
Identify, remove, pack, transport, or dispose of hazardous materials, including asbestos, lead-based paint, waste oil, fuel, transmission fluid, radioactive materials, and contaminated soil. **Skill levels:** *High:* Mechanical, science. *Basic:* Communication, interpersonal, mathematics. *Not essential:* Artistic, managerial. **Education and training:** Moderate-term on-the-job training. **Annual earnings:** $33,320. **Annual openings:** 8,000. **Job growth through 2012:** 43.1%.

❑ **Insulation Workers**
Line and cover structures with insulating materials to help control and maintain temperature. May work with batt, roll, or blown insulation materials. **Skill levels:** *High:* Mechanical. *Basic:* Communication, interpersonal, mathematics, science. *Not essential:* Artistic, managerial. **Education and training:** Moderate-term on-the-job training. **Annual earnings:** $31,265. **Annual openings:** 9,000. **Job growth through 2012:** 15.8%.

❑ **Material Moving Occupations**
Use machinery to move construction materials, earth, petroleum products, and other heavy materials, generally over short distances; manually handle freight, stock, or other materials; clean equipment; or feed materials into processing machinery. **Skill levels:** *High:* Mechanical. *Basic:* Communication. *Not essential:* Artistic, interpersonal, managerial, mathematics, science. **Education and training:** Moderate-term on-the-job training. **Annual earnings:** $26,896. **Annual openings:** 930,000. **Job growth through 2012:** −1.5%.

❑ **Painters and Paperhangers**
Paint walls, equipment, buildings, bridges, and other structural surfaces using brushes, rollers, and spray guns, or cover interior walls and ceilings of rooms with decorative wallpaper or fabric. **Skill levels:** *High:* Mechanical. *Moderate:* Artistic. *Basic:* Communication, interpersonal, mathematics, science. *Not essential:* Managerial. **Education and training:** Moderate-term on-the-job training. **Annual earnings:** $30,366. **Annual openings:** 72,000. **Job growth through 2012:** 11.4%.

❑ **Pipelayers, Plumbers, Pipefitters, and Steamfitters**
Assemble, install, alter, and repair pipelines or pipe systems that carry water, steam, air, or other liquids or gases. May install heating and cooling equipment and mechanical control systems. **Skill levels:** *High:* Mechanical. *Moderate:* Science. *Basic:* Communication, interpersonal, mathematics. *Not essential:* Artistic, managerial. **Education and training:** Long-term on-the-job training. **Annual earnings:** $39,936. **Annual openings:** 62,000. **Job growth through 2012:** 18.0%.

❑ **Plasterers and Stucco Masons**
Apply interior or exterior plaster, cement, stucco, or similar materials. May also set ornamental plaster. **Skill levels:** *High:* Mechanical. *Basic:* Artistic, communication, interpersonal, mathematics, science. *Not essential:* Managerial. **Education and training:** Long-term on-the-job training. **Annual earnings:** $32,440. **Annual openings:** 8,000. **Job growth through 2012:** 13.5%.

❑ **Roofers**
Cover roofs of structures with shingles, slate, asphalt, aluminum, wood, and related materials. May spray roofs, sidings, and walls with material to bind, seal, insulate, or soundproof sections of structures. **Skill levels:** *High:* Mechanical. *Basic:* Artistic, communication, interpersonal, mathematics, science. *Not essential:* Managerial. **Education and training:** Moderate-term on-the-job training. **Annual earnings:** $30,840. **Annual openings:** 38,000. **Job growth through 2012:** 18.6%.

❑ **Sheet Metal Workers**
Fabricate, assemble, install, and repair sheet metal products and equipment, such as ducts, control boxes, drainpipes, and furnace casings. **Skill levels:** *High:* Mechanical. *Basic:* Artistic, communication, interpersonal, mathematics, science. *Not essential:* Managerial. **Education and training:** Moderate-term on-the-job training. **Annual earnings:** $35,560. **Annual openings:** 30,000. **Job growth through 2012:** 19.8%.

❑ **Structural and Reinforcing Iron and Metal Workers**
Place and install iron or steel girders, columns, and other construction materials to form buildings, bridges, and other structures. Position and secure steel bars or mesh in concrete forms to reinforce concrete. **Skill levels:** *High:* Mechanical. *Basic:* Artistic, communication, interpersonal, mathematics, science. *Not essential:* Managerial. **Education and training:** Long-term on-the-job training. **Annual earnings:** $40,460. **Annual openings:** 11,000. **Job growth through 2012:** 16.1%.

Systems and Equipment Installation, Maintenance, and Repair

❑ **Electrical and Electronic Installers and Repairers**

Install, maintain, and repair complex electronic equipment. Use software programs and testing equipment to diagnose malfunctions. Use hand tools to replace faulty parts and adjust equipment. **Skill levels:** *High:* Mechanical. *Moderate:* Mathematics. *Basic:* Communication, interpersonal, science. *Not essential:* Artistic, managerial. **Education and training:** Postsecondary vocational award. **Annual earnings:** $40,186. **Annual openings:** 18,000. **Job growth through 2012:** 8.2%.

❑ **Elevator Installers and Repairers**

Assemble, install, repair, or maintain electric or hydraulic freight or passenger elevators, escalators, or dumbwaiters. **Skill levels:** *High:* Mechanical. *Basic:* Communication, interpersonal, mathematics, science. *Not essential:* Artistic, managerial. **Education and training:** Long-term on-the-job training. **Annual earnings:** $58,710. **Annual openings:** 3,000. **Job growth through 2012:** 17.1%.

❑ **Heating, Air Conditioning, and Refrigeration Mechanics and Installers**

Install or repair heating, central air conditioning, or refrigeration systems, including oil burners, hot-air furnaces, and heating stoves. **Skill levels:** *High:* Mechanical. *Basic:* Communication, interpersonal, mathematics, science. *Not essential:* Artistic, managerial. **Education and training:** Long-term on-the-job training. **Annual earnings:** $36,260. Annual openings: 35,000. **Job growth through 2012:** 31.8%

❑ **Home Appliance Repairers**

Repair, adjust, or install all types of electric or gas household appliances, such as refrigerators, washers, dryers, and ovens. **Skill levels:** *High:* Mechanical. *Basic:* Communication, interpersonal, mathematics, science. *Not essential:* Artistic, managerial. **Education and training:** Long-term on-the-job training. **Annual earnings:** $32,180. **Annual openings:** 5,000. **Job growth through 2012:** 5.5%.

❑ **Industrial Machinery Installation, Repair, and Maintenance Workers, Except Millwrights**

Repair, install, adjust, or maintain industrial production and processing machinery or refinery and pipeline distribution systems. **Skill levels:** *High:* Mechanical. *Basic:* Communication, mathematics, science. *Not essential:* Artistic, interpersonal, managerial. **Education and training:** Moderate-term

on-the-job training. **Annual earnings:** $31,894. **Annual openings:** 22,262.
Job growth through 2012: 14.3%.

❑ **Line Installers and Repairers**
Install or repair cables or wires used in systems that distribute electrical
power or telephone, television, or Internet communications. May erect
poles and light or heavy duty transmission towers. **Skill levels:** *High:*
Mechanical. *Moderate:* Mathematics. *Basic:* Communication, science. *Not
essential:* Artistic, interpersonal, managerial. **Education and training:** Long-
term on-the-job training. **Annual earnings:** $43,635. **Annual openings:**
22,000. **Job growth through 2012:** 12.3%.

❑ **Maintenance and Repair Workers, General**
Perform work involving the skills of two or more maintenance or craft
occupations to keep machines, mechanical equipment, or the structure
of an establishment in repair. **Skill levels:** *High:* Mechanical. *Basic:*
Communication, interpersonal, mathematics, science. *Not essential:* artistic,
managerial. **Education and training:** Moderate-term on-the-job training.
Annual earnings: $30,710. **Annual openings:** 155,000. **Job growth
through 2012:** 16.3%.

❑ **Radio and Telecommunications Equipment Installers and Repairers**
Set up and maintain equipment such as switches and cables in central
telecommunications offices, private branch exchange (PBX) switchboards,
telephone wiring and equipment on customers' premises, and radio transmitting and receiving equipment. **Skill levels:** *High:* Mechanical. *Moderate:*
Mathematics, science. *Basic:* Communication, interpersonal. *Not essential:*
Artistic, managerial. **Education and training:** Long-term on-the-job training. **Annual earnings:** $49,434. **Annual openings:** 24,000. **Job growth
through 2012:** −1.5%.

Construction Support/Labor

❑ **Construction Laborers**
Perform a wide range of physically demanding tasks involving building and
highway construction, tunnel and shaft excavation, hazardous waste
removal, environmental remediation, and demolition. **Skill levels:** *High:*
Mechanical. *Basic:* Artistic, communication, interpersonal, mathematics,
science. *Not essential:* Managerial. **Education and training:** Moderate-term
on-the-job training. **Annual earnings:** $25,160. **Annual openings:**
166,000. **Job growth through 2012:** 14.2%.

3. Arts and Communication

Managerial Work in Arts and Communication

❑ **Actors, Producers, and Directors**

Play parts in stage, television, radio, video, or motion picture productions for entertainment, information, or instruction, or produce or direct stage, television, radio, video, or motion picture productions. **Skill levels:** *High:* Artistic, communication, interpersonal. *Moderate:* Managerial, mechanical. *Basic:* Science. *Not essential:* Mathematics. **Education and training:** Bachelor's or higher degree, plus work experience (does not apply to Actors). **Annual earnings:** $52,840 (does not apply to Actors). **Annual openings:** 18,000. **Job growth through 2012:** 18.0%.

❑ **Advertising, Marketing, Promotions, Public Relations, and Sales Managers**

Coordinate market research, marketing strategy, sales, advertising, promotion, pricing, product development, and public relations activities. Oversee advertising and promotion staffs. **Skill levels:** *High:* Artistic, communication, interpersonal, managerial, mathematics. *Moderate:* Mechanical. *Not essential:* Science. **Education and training:** Work experience plus degree. **Annual earnings:** $82,252. **Annual openings:** 107,000. **Job growth through 2012:** 26.5%.

❑ **Artists and Related Workers**

Create art to communicate ideas, thoughts, or feelings. May formulate design concepts and presentation approaches for media or create original artwork using a variety of media and techniques. **Skill levels:** *High:* Artistic. *Moderate:* Mechanical. *Basic:* Communication, interpersonal, managerial, mathematics, science. **Education and training:** Bachelor's degree. **Annual earnings:** $53,075. **Annual openings:** 24,000. **Job growth through 2012:** 14.4%.

Writing and Editing

❑ **Writers and Editors**

Develop original fiction and nonfiction for publication, examine proposals and select material for publication or broadcast, review and revise a writer's work for publication or dissemination, or develop technical materials such as manuals. **Skill levels:** *High:* Artistic, communication, interpersonal. *Basic:* Managerial, mathematics, science. *Not essential:* Mechanical.

Education and training: Bachelor's degree. **Annual earnings:** $45,595.
Annual openings: 43,000. **Job growth through 2012:** 16.1%.

News, Broadcasting, and Public Relations

❏ **Interpreters and Translators**

Convert one spoken language into another, interpret between spoken
communication and sign language, or convert written materials from one
language into another. **Skill levels:** *High:* Artistic, communication. *Basic:*
Interpersonal. *Not essential:* Managerial, mathematics, mechanical, science.
Education and training: Long-term on-the-job training. **Annual earnings:**
$33,860. **Annual openings:** 4,000. **Job growth through 2012:** 22.1%.

❏ **News Analysts, Reporters, and Correspondents**

Collect and analyze facts about newsworthy events by interview, investiga-
tion, or observation. Report and write stories for newspaper, news maga-
zine, radio, or television. **Skill levels:** *High:* Communication, interpersonal.
Moderate: Artistic, science. *Basic:* Managerial, mathematics, mechanical.
Education and training: Bachelor's degree. **Annual earnings:** $31,979.
Annual openings: 6,000. **Job growth through 2012:** 6.2%.

❏ **Public Relations Specialists**

Engage in promoting or creating good will for individuals, groups, or
organizations by writing or selecting favorable publicity material and
releasing it through various communications media. May prepare and
arrange displays and make speeches. **Skill levels:** *High:* Communication,
interpersonal. *Moderate:* Artistic. *Basic:* Managerial, mathematics.
Not essential: Mechanical, science. **Education and training:** Bachelor's
degree. **Annual earnings:** $43,830. **Annual openings:** 28,000. **Job growth
through 2012:** 32.9%.

Design

❏ **Designers**

Combine practical knowledge with artistic ability to turn abstract ideas
into formal designs. Determine the needs of the client, the function for
which the design is intended, and its appeal to customers or users. Create
models or representations. **Skill levels:** *High:* Artistic, managerial, mechanical. *Moderate:* Communication, interpersonal. *Basic:* Mathematics, science.
Education and training: Bachelor's degree. **Annual earnings:** $34,514.
Annual openings: 71,000. **Job growth through 2012:** 17.4%.

Drama

❑ **Actors, Producers, and Directors**

Play parts in stage, television, radio, video, or motion picture productions for entertainment, information, or instruction, or produce or direct stage, television, radio, video, or motion picture productions. **Skill levels:** *High:* Artistic, communication, interpersonal. *Moderate:* Managerial, mechanical. *Basic:* Science. *Not essential:* Mathematics. **Education and training:** Work experience plus degree. **Annual earnings:** $52,840. **Annual openings:** 18,000. **Job growth through 2012:** 18.0%.

❑ **Announcers**

Talk on radio or television or make announcements over loudspeaker at sporting or other public events. **Skill levels:** *High:* Communication, interpersonal. *Moderate:* Artistic. *Basic:* Mathematics, mechanical. *Not essential:* Managerial, science. **Education and training:** Associate's degree. **Annual earnings:** $22,102. **Annual openings:** 8,000. **Job growth through 2012:** −10.1%.

Music

❑ **Musicians, Singers, and Related Workers**

Play musical instruments, sing, compose or arrange music, or conduct groups in instrumental or vocal performances. May perform solo or as part of a group. **Skill levels:** *High:* Artistic. *Moderate:* Communication, interpersonal. *Basic:* Managerial, mechanical, science. *Not essential:* Mathematics. **Education and training:** Bachelor's or higher degree, plus work experience (applies only to Music Directors and Composers). **Annual earnings:** $34,570 (applies only to Music Directors and Composers). **Annual openings:** 33,000. **Job growth through 2012:** 16.2%.

Dance

❑ **Dancers and Choreographers**

Perform dances or create and teach dance. **Skill levels:** *High:* Artistic. *Moderate:* Communication, interpersonal, managerial. *Basic:* Science. *Not essential:* Mathematics, mechanical. **Education and training:** Work experience in a related occupation (applies only to Choreographers). **Annual earnings:** $33,670 (applies only to Choreographers). **Annual openings:** 6,000. **Job growth through 2012:** 13.3%.

Media Technology

❑ **Broadcast and Sound Engineering Technicians and Radio Operators**
Set up, operate, and maintain a wide variety of electrical and electronic equipment involved in almost any radio or television broadcast, concert, play, musical recording, television show, or movie. **Skill levels:** *High:* Mechanical. *Moderate:* Interpersonal, mathematics, science. *Basic:* Communication. *Not essential:* Artistic, managerial. **Education and training:** Moderate-term on-the-job training. **Annual earnings:** $31,633. **Annual openings:** 11,000. **Job growth through 2012:** 19.7%.

❑ **Photographers**
Photograph persons, subjects, merchandise, or commercial products. May develop negatives and produce finished prints. **Skill levels:** *High:* Artistic, mechanical. *Basic:* Communication, interpersonal, managerial, mathematics, science. **Education and training:** Long-term on-the-job training. **Annual earnings:** $26,080. **Annual openings:** 18,000. **Job growth through 2012:** 13.6%.

❑ **Photographic Process Workers and Processing Machine Operators**
Perform precision work involved in photographic processing, such as editing photographic negatives and prints; using photo-mechanical, chemical, or computerized methods; or operating photographic processing machines. **Skill levels:** *High:* Mechanical. *Basic:* Artistic, communication, mathematics, science. *Not essential:* Interpersonal, managerial. **Education and training:** Short-term on-the-job training. **Annual earnings:** $19,619. **Annual openings:** 13,000. **Job growth through 2012:** 7.9%.

❑ **Television, Video, and Motion Picture Camera Operators and Editors**
Operate video equipment to produce images that tell a story, inform or entertain an audience, or record an event. May edit soundtracks, film, and video for the motion picture, cable, and broadcast television industries. **Skill levels:** *High:* Artistic, mechanical. *Basic:* Communication, interpersonal, managerial, mathematics, science. **Education and training:** Moderate-term on-the-job training. **Annual earnings:** $40,027. **Annual openings:** 7,000. **Job growth through 2012:** 18.7%.

Communications Technology

❑ **Air Traffic Controllers**
Control air traffic on and within vicinity of airport and movement of air traffic between altitude sectors and control centers according to established

procedures and policies. **Skill levels:** *High:* Communication. *Moderate:* Interpersonal, managerial, mathematics, science. *Not essential:* Artistic, mechanical. **Education and training:** Long-term on-the-job training. **Annual earnings:** $102,030. **Annual openings:** 2,000. **Job growth through 2012:** 12.6%.

❑ **Communications Equipment Operators**
Operate telephone business systems equipment or switchboards to relay incoming, outgoing, and interoffice calls, or supply information, emergency response, or billing request services to callers. **Skill levels:** *Moderate:* Communication, interpersonal, mathematics, mechanical. *Basic:* Science. *Not essential:* Artistic, managerial. **Education and training:** Short-term on-the-job training. **Annual earnings:** $22,772. **Annual openings:** 54,000. **Job growth through 2012:** –9.6%.

❑ **Dispatchers**
Schedule and dispatch workers, equipment, or service vehicles for the conveyance of materials or passengers. Keep records, logs, and schedules of calls, transportation vehicles, and actions taken. **Skill levels:** *Moderate:* Communication, managerial. *Basic:* Interpersonal, mathematics. *Not essential:* Artistic, mechanical, science. **Education and training:** Moderate-term on-the-job training. **Annual earnings:** $30,221. **Annual openings:** 43,000. **Job growth through 2012:** 13.8%.

❑ **Material Recording, Scheduling, Dispatching, and Distributing Occupations**
Coordinate, expedite, and track orders for personnel, materials, and equipment. **Skill levels:** *Basic:* Communication, interpersonal, mathematics, mechanical. *Not essential:* Artistic, managerial, science. **Education and training:** Short-term on-the-job training. **Annual earnings:** $26,930. **Annual openings:** 768,000. **Job growth through 2012:** 0.6%.

Musical Instrument Repair

❑ **Precision Instrument and Equipment Repairers**
Repair and maintain watches, cameras, musical instruments, medical equipment, or other precision instruments. May machine or fabricate a new part. For preventive maintenance may perform regular lubrication, cleaning, and adjustment. **Skill levels:** *High:* Mechanical. *Moderate:* Mathematics. *Basic:* Artistic, communication, science. *Not essential:* Interpersonal, managerial. **Education and training:** Associate degree. **Annual earnings:** $34,427. **Annual openings:** 7,000. **Job growth through 2012:** 9.3%.

4. Business and Administration

Managerial Work in General Business

❑ Human Resources, Training, and Labor Relations Managers and Specialists

Handle employee benefits questions. Recruit, interview, and hire new personnel in accordance with policies and requirements that have been established in conjunction with top management. Consult with top executives regarding strategic planning. **Skill levels:** *High:* Communication, interpersonal, managerial. *Basic:* Mathematics. *Not essential:* Artistic, mechanical, science. **Education and training:** Bachelor's degree. **Annual earnings:** $50,641. **Annual openings:** 100,000. **Job growth through 2012:** 25.2%.

❑ Top Executives

Devise strategies and formulate policies to ensure that a business, corporation, nonprofit institution, government, or other organization meets its objectives. **Skill levels:** *High:* Communication, interpersonal, managerial, mathematics. *Moderate:* Science. *Basic:* Artistic. *Not essential:* Mechanical. **Education and training:** Work experience plus degree. **Annual earnings:** $88,922. **Annual openings:** 327,000. **Job growth through 2012:** 17.6%.

Managerial Work in Business Detail

❑ Administrative Service Managers

Plan, direct, or coordinate supportive services of an organization, such as recordkeeping, mail distribution, telephone operator/receptionist, and other office support services. May oversee facilities planning and maintenance and custodial operations. **Skill levels:** *High:* Communication, interpersonal, managerial. *Moderate:* Mathematics. *Basic:* Artistic. *Not essential:* Mechanical, science. **Education and training:** Work experience plus degree. **Annual earnings:** $60,290. **Annual openings:** 40,000. **Job growth through 2012:** 19.8%.

❑ Office and Administrative Support Supervisors and Managers

Supervise and coordinate the activities of clerical and administrative support workers. **Skill levels:** *High:* Communication, interpersonal, managerial. *Moderate:* Mathematics. *Basic:* Mechanical. *Not essential:* Artistic, science. **Education and training:** Work experience in a related occupation. **Annual earnings:** $41,030. **Annual openings:** 140,000. **Job growth through 2012:** 6.6%.

Human Resources Support

❏ **Human Resources, Training, and Labor Relations Managers and Specialists**

Handle employee benefits questions. Recruit, interview, and hire new personnel in accordance with policies and requirements that have been established in conjunction with top management. Consult with top executives regarding strategic planning. **Skill levels:** *High:* Communication, interpersonal, managerial. *Basic:* Mathematics. *Not essential:* Artistic, mechanical, science. **Education and training:** Bachelor's degree. **Annual earnings:** $50,641. **Annual openings:** 100,000. **Job growth through 2012:** 25.2%.

Secretarial Support

❏ **Secretaries and Administrative Assistants**

Provide administrative support by conducting research, preparing statistical reports, handling information requests, and performing clerical functions. **Skill levels:** *High:* Communication, interpersonal. *Basic:* Artistic, managerial, mathematics. *Not essential:* Mechanical, science. **Education and training:** Moderate-term on-the-job training. **Annual earnings:** $30,122. **Annual openings:** 553,000. **Job growth through 2012:** 4.5%.

Accounting, Auditing, and Analytical Support

❏ **Accountants and Auditors**

Examine, analyze, and interpret accounting records for the purpose of giving advice or preparing statements. Install or advise on systems of recording costs or other financial and budgetary data. **Skill levels:** *High:* Mathematics. *Moderate:* Managerial. *Basic:* Communication, interpersonal. *Not essential:* Artistic, mechanical, science. **Education and training:** Bachelor's degree. **Annual earnings:** $50,770. **Annual openings:** 119,000. **Job growth through 2012:** 19.5%.

❏ **Budget Analysts**

Examine budget estimates for completeness, accuracy, and conformance with procedures and regulations. Analyze budgeting and accounting reports for the purpose of maintaining expenditure controls. **Skill levels:** *High:* Mathematics. *Basic:* Communication, interpersonal, managerial. *Not essential:* Artistic, mechanical, science. **Education and training:** Bachelor's degree. **Annual earnings:** $56,040. **Annual openings:** 8,000. **Job growth through 2012:** 14.0%.

❑ **Engineering Technicians**
Use the principles and theories of science, engineering, and mathematics to solve technical problems in research and development, manufacturing, sales, construction, inspection, and maintenance. **Skill levels:** *High:* Mathematics, mechanical, science. *Moderate:* Communication. *Basic:* Artistic, interpersonal. *Not essential:* Managerial. **Education and training:** Associate degree. **Annual earnings:** $43,685. **Annual openings:** 56,000. **Job growth through 2012:** 10.0%.

❑ **Management Analysts**
Conduct organizational studies and evaluations, design systems and procedures, conduct work simplifications and measurement studies, and prepare operations and procedures manuals to assist management in operating more efficiently and effectively. **Skill levels:** *High:* Communication, mathematics. *Moderate:* Interpersonal. *Basic:* Managerial. *Not essential:* Artistic, mechanical, science. **Education and training:** Work experience plus degree. **Annual earnings:** $63,450. **Annual openings:** 78,000. **Job growth through 2012:** 30.4%.

❑ **Operations Research Analysts**
Formulate and apply mathematical modeling and other optimizing methods using a computer to develop and interpret information that assists management with decision making, policy formulation, or other managerial functions. **Skill levels:** *High:* Mathematics. *Moderate:* Science. *Basic:* Communication, interpersonal, managerial. *Not essential:* Artistic, mechanical. **Education and training:** Master's degree. **Annual earnings:** $60,190. **Annual openings:** 6,000. **Job growth through 2012:** 6.2%.

Mathematical Clerical Support

❑ **Billing and Posting Clerks and Machine Operators**
Compile, compute, and record billing, accounting, statistical, and other numerical data for billing purposes. Prepare billing invoices for services rendered or for delivery or shipment of goods. **Skill levels:** *Basic:* Communication, interpersonal, mathematics, mechanical. *Not essential:* Artistic, managerial, science. **Education and training:** Moderate-term on-the-job training. **Annual earnings:** $27,040. **Annual openings:** 78,000. **Job growth through 2012:** 7.9%.

❑ **Bookkeeping, Accounting, and Auditing Clerks**
Compute, classify, and record numerical data to keep financial records complete. Perform any combination of routine calculating, posting, and

verifying duties to obtain primary financial data. **Skill levels:** *High:* Mathematics. *Basic:* Communication, interpersonal. *Not essential:* Artistic, managerial, mechanical, science. **Education and training:** Moderate-term on-the-job training. **Annual earnings:** $28,570. **Annual openings:** 274,000. **Job growth through 2012:** 3.0%.

❑ **Brokerage Clerks**

Perform clerical duties involving the purchase or sale of securities. Duties include writing orders for stock purchases and sales, computing transfer taxes, verifying stock transactions, accepting and delivering securities, and tracking stocks. **Skill levels:** *Moderate:* Mathematics. *Basic:* Communication, interpersonal. *Not essential:* Artistic, managerial, mechanical, science. **Education and training:** Moderate-term on-the-job training. **Annual earnings:** $35,240. **Annual openings:** 10,000. **Job growth through 2012:** –14.7%.

❑ **Financial Clerks**

Keep track of money, recording all amounts coming into or leaving an organization. Work in offices, maintaining and processing various accounting records, or deal directly with customers, taking in and paying out money. **Skill levels:** *High:* Mathematics. *Basic:* Communication, interpersonal. *Not essential:* Artistic, managerial, mechanical, science. **Education and training:** Moderate-term on-the-job training. **Annual earnings:** $27,290. **Annual openings:** 594,000. **Job growth through 2012:** 7.0%.

❑ **Information and Record Clerks**

Gather data and provide information to the public. Greet customers, guests, or other visitors. May answer telephones. **Skill levels:** *Moderate:* Communication, mathematics. *Basic:* Interpersonal. *Not essential:* Artistic, managerial, mechanical, science. **Education and training:** Moderate-term on-the-job training. **Annual earnings:** $26,402. **Annual openings:** 585,000. **Job growth through 2012:** 17.8%.

❑ **Payroll and Timekeeping Clerks**

Compile and post employee time and payroll data. May compute employees' time worked, production, and commission. May compute and post wages and deductions. May prepare paychecks. **Skill levels:** *Moderate:* Mathematics. *Basic:* Communication, interpersonal. *Not essential:* Artistic, managerial, mechanical, science. **Education and training:** Moderate-term on-the-job training. **Annual earnings:** $30,350. **Annual openings:** 19,000. **Job growth through 2012:** 6.5%.

Records and Materials Processing

❑ **File Clerks**

File correspondence, cards, invoices, receipts, and other records in alphabetical or numerical order or according to the filing system used. **Skill levels:** *Basic:* Communication, interpersonal, mathematics. *Not essential:* Artistic, managerial, mechanical, science. **Education and training:** Short-term on-the-job training. **Annual openings:** 62,000. **Annual earnings:** $21,030. **Job growth through 2012:** –0.3%.

❑ **Human Resources Assistants, except Payroll and Timekeeping**

Compile and keep personnel records. Record data for each employee, such as address, weekly earnings, absences, amount of sales or production, supervisory reports on ability, and date of and reason for termination. **Skill levels:** *Moderate:* Mathematics. *Basic:* Communication, interpersonal. *Not essential:* Artistic, managerial, mechanical, science. **Education and training:** Short-term on-the-job training. **Annual openings:** 36,000. **Annual earnings:** $31,750. **Job growth through 2012:** 19.3%.

❑ **Material Recording, Scheduling, Dispatching, and Distributing Occupations**

Coordinate, expedite, and track orders for personnel, materials, and equipment. **Skill levels:** *Basic:* Communication, interpersonal, mathematics, mechanical. *Not essential:* Artistic, managerial, science. **Education and training:** Short-term on-the-job training. **Annual earnings:** $26,930. **Annual openings:** 768,000. **Job growth through 2012:** 0.6%.

❑ **Meter Readers, Utilities**

Read electric, gas, water, or steam consumption meters and record the volume used. **Skill levels:** *Moderate:* Mathematics. *Basic:* Communication, mechanical. *Not essential:* Artistic, interpersonal, managerial, science. **Education and training:** Short-term on-the-job training. **Annual earnings:** $29,440. **Annual openings:** 10,000. **Job growth through 2012:** –14.1%.

❑ **Office Clerks, General**

Perform duties too varied and diverse to be classified in any specific office clerical occupation; requires limited knowledge of office management systems and procedures. **Skill levels:** *Moderate:* Interpersonal. *Basic:* Communication, mathematics. *Not essential:* Artistic, managerial, mechanical, science. **Education and training:** Short-term on-the-job training. **Annual earnings:** $22,770. **Annual openings:** 550,000. **Job growth through 2012:** 10.4%.

❑ **Postal Service Workers**
Deliver mail or perform any combination of tasks in a post office, such as receive letters and parcels, sell postage stamps, fill out and sell money orders, and place mail in pigeon holes of mail rack. **Skill levels:** *Basic:* Communication, interpersonal, managerial, mechanical. *Not essential:* Artistic, science. **Education and training:** Short-term on-the-job training. **Annual earnings:** $42,131. **Annual openings:** 43,000. **Job growth through 2012:** –4.3%.

❑ **Procurement Clerks**
Perform a variety of tasks related to the ordering of goods and supplies for an organization and make sure that what was purchased arrives on schedule and meets the purchaser's specifications. **Skill levels:** *Moderate:* Mathematics. *Basic:* Communication, interpersonal. *Not essential:* Artistic, managerial, mechanical, science. **Education and training:** Short-term on-the-job training. **Annual earnings:** $30,890. **Annual openings:** 13,000. **Job growth through 2012:** –6.7%.

❑ **Production, Planning, and Expediting Clerks**
Coordinate and expedite the flow of information, work, and materials within or among offices. **Skill levels:** *Moderate:* Communication, mathematics. *Basic:* Interpersonal, managerial, science. *Not essential:* Artistic, mechanical. **Education and training:** Short-term on-the-job training. **Annual earnings:** $36,340. **Annual openings:** 51,000. **Job growth through 2012:** 14.1%.

❑ **Shipping, Receiving, and Traffic Clerks**
Verify and keep records on incoming and outgoing shipments. Prepare items for shipment. **Skill levels:** *Moderate:* Mechanical. *Basic:* Communication, interpersonal, mathematics. *Not essential:* Artistic, managerial, science. **Education and training:** Short-term on-the-job training. **Annual earnings:** $24,400. **Annual openings:** 154,000. **Job growth through 2012:** 3.0%.

❑ **Stock Clerks and Order Fillers**
Receive, unpack, check, store, and track merchandise or materials. Keep records of items entering or leaving the stockroom and inspect damaged or spoiled goods. Sort, organize, and mark items with identifying codes. **Skill levels:** *Basic:* Communication, interpersonal, mathematics, mechanical. *Not essential:* Artistic, managerial, science. **Education and training:** Short-term on-the-job training. **Annual earnings:** $20,100. **Annual openings:** 418,000. **Job growth through 2012:** –4.2%.

❑ **Weighers, Measurers, Checkers, and Samplers, Recordkeeping**
Weigh, measure, and check materials, supplies, and equipment in order
to keep relevant records. **Skill levels:** *Moderate:* Mathematics, mechanical,
science. *Basic:* Communication, interpersonal. *Not essential:* Artistic, managerial. **Education and training:** Short-term on-the-job training. **Annual
earnings:** $24,570. **Annual openings:** 16,000. **Job growth through 2012:**
14.6%.

Clerical Machine Operation

❑ **Billing and Posting Clerks and Machine Operators**
Compile, compute, and record billing, accounting, statistical, and other
numerical data for billing purposes. Prepare billing invoices for services
rendered or for delivery or shipment of goods. **Skill levels:** *Basic:*
Communication, interpersonal, mathematics, mechanical. *Not essential:*
Artistic, managerial, science. **Education and training:** Moderate-term on-
the-job training. **Annual earnings:** $27,040. **Annual openings:** 78,000.
Job growth through 2012: 7.9%.

❑ **Communications Equipment Operators**
Operate telephone business systems equipment or switchboards to relay
incoming, outgoing, and interoffice calls, or supply information, emer-
gency response, or billing request services to callers. **Skill levels:** *Moderate:*
Communication, interpersonal, mathematics, mechanical. *Basic:* Science.
Not essential: Artistic, managerial. **Education and training:** Short-term on-
the-job training. **Annual earnings:** $22,772. **Annual openings:** 54,000.
Job growth through 2012: –9.6%.

❑ **Data Entry and Information Processing Workers**
Type text, enter data into a computer, operate a variety of office machines,
and perform other clerical duties. **Skill levels:** *Moderate:* Mechanical. *Basic:*
Communication, interpersonal, mathematics. *Not essential:* Artistic, managerial, science. **Education and training:** Moderate-term on-the-job training. **Annual earnings:** $33,670. **Annual openings:** 117,000. **Job growth
through 2012:** –18.0%.

5. Education and Training

Managerial Work in Education

❑ **Education Administrators**
Plan, direct, or coordinate the academic and nonacademic activities of
an educational institution, or may direct the educational programs of a

business, correctional institution, museum, or job training facility. **Skill levels:** *High:* Communication, interpersonal, managerial. *Moderate:* Mathematics. *Basic:* Science. *Not essential:* Artistic, mechanical. **Education and training:** Work experience plus degree. **Annual earnings:** $66,785. **Annual openings:** 59,000. **Job growth through 2012:** 24.0%.

❑ **Instructional Coordinators**
Develop instructional materials, train teachers, and assess educational programs in terms of quality and adherence to regulations and standards. Assist in implementing new technology in the classroom. **Skill levels:** *High:* Communication, interpersonal. *Moderate:* Managerial, mathematics, mechanical, science. *Basic:* Artistic. **Education and training:** Master's degree. **Annual earnings:** $48,790. **Annual openings:** 18,000. **Job growth through 2012:** 25.4%.

Preschool, Elementary, and Secondary Teaching and Instructing

❑ **Teacher Assistants**
Perform duties that are instructional in nature or deliver direct services to students or parents. Serve in a position for which a teacher or another professional has ultimate responsibility for the design and implementation of educational programs. **Skill levels:** *High:* Communication, interpersonal. *Moderate:* Artistic, managerial, science. *Basic:* Mathematics. *Not essential:* Mechanical. **Education and training:** Short-term on-the-job training. **Annual earnings:** $19,410. **Annual openings:** 259,000. **Job growth through 2012:** 23.0%.

❑ **Teacher—Preschool, Kindergarten, Elementary, Middle, and Secondary**
Help students learn and apply concepts in subjects such as science, mathematics, or English. Help children understand abstract concepts, solve problems, and develop critical thought processes. **Skill levels:** *High:* Communication, interpersonal, managerial. *Moderate:* Artistic, mathematics, science. *Basic:* Mechanical. **Education and training:** Work experience plus degree. **Annual earnings:** $41,393. **Annual openings:** 506,000. **Job growth through 2012:** 17.7%.

❑ **Teacher—Special Education**
Work with children and youths who have a variety of disabilities. May use the general education curriculum or modify it to meet the learner's individual needs. **Skill levels:** *High:* Communication, interpersonal, managerial. *Moderate:* Artistic, mathematics, science. *Basic:* Mechanical. **Education and**

training: Bachelor's degree. **Annual earnings:** $44,367. **Annual openings:** 23,000. **Job growth through 2012:** 30.0%.

Postsecondary and Adult Teaching and Instructing

❑ Teacher—Postsecondary

Instruct students in a wide variety of academic and vocational subjects beyond the high school level that may lead to a degree or simply to improvement in one's knowledge or skills. **Skill levels:** *High:* Communication, interpersonal, managerial, mathematics. *Moderate:* Artistic, science. *Not essential:* Mechanical. **Education and training:** Master's degree. **Annual earnings:** $42,799. **Annual openings:** 96,000. **Job growth through 2012:** 38.1%.

❑ Teachers—Adult Literacy and Remedial and Self-Enrichment Education

Teach courses that students take for pleasure or personal enrichment (rather than to lead to a particular degree or vocation), or provide adults and out-of-school youths with the education they need to read, write, and speak English. **Skill levels:** *High:* Communication, interpersonal, managerial. *Moderate:* Artistic, mathematics, science. *Not essential:* Mechanical. **Education and training:** Bachelor's degree. **Annual earnings:** $38,980. **Annual openings:** 14,000. **Job growth through 2012:** 20.4%.

Library Services

❑ Librarians

Administer libraries and perform related library services. Select, acquire, catalogue, classify, circulate, and maintain library materials. Furnish reference, bibliographical, and readers' advisory services. **Skill levels:** *High:* Communication, managerial. *Moderate:* Interpersonal, mechanical. *Basic:* Artistic, mathematics, science. **Education and training:** Master's degree. **Annual earnings:** $45,900. **Annual openings:** 15,000. **Job growth through 2012:** 10.1%.

❑ Library Assistants, Clerical

Compile records, sort and shelve books, and issue and receive library materials. Locate library materials for loan and replace material in shelving area, stacks, or files. **Skill levels:** *Moderate:* Mechanical. *Basic:* Communication, interpersonal, mathematics, science. *Not essential:* Artistic, managerial. **Education and training:** Short-term on-the-job training. **Annual earnings:** $20,720. **Annual openings:** 27,000. **Job growth through 2012:** 21.5%.

❏ **Library Technicians**

Assist librarians by helping readers in the use of library catalogs, databases, and indexes to locate books and other materials and by answering questions that require only brief consultation of standard reference. **Skill levels:** *Moderate:* Communication, mechanical. *Basic:* Artistic, interpersonal, managerial, mathematics, science. **Education and training:** Short-term on-the-job training. **Annual earnings:** $24,940. **Annual openings:** 22,000. **Job growth through 2012:** 16.8%.

Archival and Museum Services

❏ **Archivists, Curators, and Museum Technicians**

Acquire and preserve important documents and other valuable items for permanent storage or display. Describe, catalogue, analyze, exhibit, and maintain valuable objects and collections for the benefit of researchers and the public. **Skill levels:** *High:* Artistic, mechanical, science. *Moderate:* Communication, mathematics. *Basic:* Interpersonal, managerial. **Education and training:** Master's degree. **Annual earnings:** $37,366. **Annual openings:** 2,000. **Job growth through 2012:** 17.0%.

Counseling, Health, and Fitness Education

❏ **Counselors**

Counsel individuals and provide group educational and vocational guidance services. Assist people with personal, family, educational, mental health, and career decisions and problems. **Skill levels:** *High:* Communication, interpersonal. *Basic:* Managerial, mathematics, science. *Not essential:* Artistic, mechanical. **Education and training:** Master's degree. **Annual earnings:** $37,411. **Annual openings:** 77,000. **Job growth through 2012:** 22.6%.

❏ **Recreation and Fitness Workers**

Conduct recreation activities with groups in public, private, or volunteer agencies or recreation facilities. Organize and promote activities, such as arts and crafts, sports, games, music, dramatics, social recreation, camping, and hobbies. **Skill levels:** *High:* Communication, interpersonal. *Basic:* Artistic, managerial, mathematics, mechanical, science. **Education and training:** Bachelor's degree. **Annual earnings:** $21,641. **Annual openings:** 94,000. **Job growth through 2012:** 29.6%.

6. Finance and Insurance

Managerial Work in Finance and Insurance

❑ Financial Managers

Plan, direct, and coordinate accounting, investing, banking, insurance, securities, and other financial activities of a branch, office, or department of an establishment. **Skill levels:** *High:* Communication, interpersonal, managerial, mathematics. *Basic:* Science. *Not essential:* Artistic, mechanical. **Education and training:** Work experience plus degree. **Annual earnings:** $81,880. **Annual openings:** 71,000. **Job growth through 2012:** 18.3%.

Finance/Insurance Investigation and Analysis

❑ Claims Adjusters, Appraisers, Examiners, and Investigators

Investigate property and casualty insurance claims, negotiate settlements, and authorize payments to claimants. Determine whether the customer's insurance policy covers the loss and how much of the loss should be paid to the claimant. **Skill levels:** *Moderate:* Communication, managerial, mathematics, mechanical. *Basic:* Interpersonal, science. *Not essential:* Artistic. **Education and training:** Long-term on-the-job training. **Annual earnings:** $44,284. **Annual openings:** 33,000. **Job growth through 2012:** 14.1%.

❑ Cost Estimators

Prepare cost estimates for product manufacturing, construction projects, or services to aid management in bidding on or determining price of product or service. May specialize according to particular service performed or type of product manufactured. **Skill levels:** *High:* Mathematics. *Basic:* Communication, interpersonal, managerial, mechanical. *Not essential:* Artistic, science. **Education and training:** Work experience in a related occupation. **Annual earnings:** $49,940. **Annual openings:** 25,000. **Job growth through 2012:** 18.6%.

❑ Financial Analysts and Personal Financial Advisors

Provide analysis and guidance to businesses and individuals to help them with their investment decisions. Gather financial information, analyze it, and make recommendations to clients. **Skill levels:** *High:* Communication, interpersonal, mathematics. *Basic:* Managerial, science. *Not essential:* Artistic, mechanical. **Education and training:** Bachelor's degree. **Annual earnings:** $62,244. **Annual openings:** 40,000. **Job growth through 2012:** 25.4%.

❑ **Insurance Underwriters**
Review individual applications for insurance to evaluate degree of risk involved and determine acceptance of applications. **Skill levels:** *High:* Mathematics. *Basic:* Communication, interpersonal, managerial. *Not essential:* Artistic, mechanical, science. **Education and training:** Bachelor's degree. **Annual earnings:** $48,550. **Annual openings:** 12,000. **Job growth through 2012:** 10.0%.

❑ **Loan Counselors and Officers**
Provide guidance to prospective loan applicants who have problems qualifying for traditional loans, or evaluate, authorize, or recommend approval of commercial, real estate, or credit loans. **Skill levels:** *High:* Interpersonal. *Moderate:* Communication, mathematics. *Basic:* Managerial. *Not essential:* Artistic, mechanical, science. **Education and training:** Bachelor's degree. **Annual earnings:** $47,016. **Annual openings:** 34,000. **Job growth through 2012:** 18.7%.

❑ **Market and Survey Researchers**
Analyze statistical data on past sales of a product or service to predict future sales. Gather data on competitors and analyze prices, sales, and methods of marketing and distribution. Devise methods and procedures for obtaining needed data. **Skill levels:** *High:* Communication, interpersonal, mathematics. *Basic:* Managerial. *Not essential:* Artistic, mechanical, science. **Education and training:** Master's degree. **Annual earnings:** $52,289. **Annual openings:** 21,000. **Job growth through 2012:** 24.7%.

Finance/Insurance Records Processing

❑ **Credit Authorizers, Checkers, and Clerks**
Authorize credit charges against customers' accounts. Investigate history and credit standing of individuals or business establishments applying for credit. **Skill levels:** *Moderate:* Communication, mathematics. *Basic:* Interpersonal, managerial. *Not essential:* Artistic, mechanical, science. **Education and training:** Short-term on-the-job training. **Annual earnings:** $29,050. **Annual openings:** 15,000. **Job growth through 2012:** –6.7%.

❑ **Information and Record Clerks**
Gather data and provide information to the public. Greet customers, guests, or other visitors. May answer telephones. **Skill levels:** *Moderate:* Communication, mathematics. *Basic:* Interpersonal. *Not essential:* Artistic, managerial, mechanical, science. **Education and training:** Moderate-term on-the-job training. **Annual earnings:** $26,402. **Annual openings:** 585,000. **Job growth through 2012:** 17.8%.

Finance/Insurance Customer Service

❑ **Bill and Account Collectors**

Locate and notify customers of delinquent accounts by mail, telephone, or personal visit to solicit payment. **Skill levels:** *High:* Interpersonal, mathematics. *Basic:* Communication. *Not essential:* Artistic, managerial, mechanical, science. **Education and training:** Short-term on-the-job training. **Annual earnings:** $27,450. **Annual openings:** 76,000. **Job growth through 2012:** 24.5%.

❑ **Financial Clerks**

Keep track of money, recording all amounts coming into or leaving an organization. Work in offices, maintaining and processing various accounting records, or deal directly with customers, taking in and paying out money. **Skill levels:** *High:* Mathematics. *Basic:* Communication, interpersonal. *Not essential:* Artistic, managerial, mechanical, science. **Education and training:** Moderate-term on-the-job training. **Annual earnings:** $27,290. **Annual openings:** 594,000. **Job growth through 2012:** 7.0%.

❑ **Interviewers**

Interview persons by telephone, mail, in person, or by other means for the purpose of completing forms, applications, or questionnaires. Ask specific questions, record answers, and assist persons with completing form. May sort, classify, and file forms. **Skill levels:** *High:* Communication. *Moderate:* Interpersonal, managerial. *Basic:* Mathematics, science. *Not essential:* Artistic, mechanical. **Education and training:** Short-term on-the-job training. **Annual earnings:** $27,594. **Annual openings:** 1,883. **Job growth through 2012:** 4.1%.

❑ **Tellers**

Receive and pay out money. Keep records of money and negotiable instruments involved in a financial institution's various transactions. **Skill levels:** *High:* Interpersonal, mathematics. *Moderate:* Communication. *Not essential:* Artistic, managerial, mechanical, science. **Education and training:** Short-term on-the-job training. **Annual earnings:** $21,120. **Annual openings:** 127,000. **Job growth through 2012:** 9.4%.

Finance/Insurance Sales and Support

❑ **Financial Analysts and Personal Financial Advisors**

Provide analysis and guidance to businesses and individuals to help them with their investment decisions. Gather financial information, analyze it, and make recommendations to clients. **Skill levels:** *High:* Communication, interpersonal, mathematics. *Basic:* Managerial, science. *Not essential:* Artistic, mechanical. **Education and training:** Bachelor's degree. **Annual earnings:** $62,244. **Annual openings:** 40,000. **Job growth through 2012:** 25.4%.

❑ **Insurance Sales Agents**
Sell life, property, casualty, health, automotive, or other types of insurance. **Skill levels:** *High:* Communication, interpersonal. *Moderate:* Mathematics. *Not essential:* Artistic, managerial, mechanical, science. **Education and training:** Bachelor's degree. **Annual earnings:** $41,720. **Annual openings:** 52,000. **Job growth through 2012:** 8.4%.

❑ **Securities, Commodities, and Financial Services Sales Agents**
Buy and sell securities in investment and trading firms, or call on businesses and individuals to sell financial services. Provide financial services, such as loan, tax, and securities counseling. **Skill levels:** *High:* Communication, interpersonal, managerial, mathematics. *Not essential:* Artistic, mechanical, science. **Education and training:** Bachelor's degree. **Annual earnings:** $69,200. **Annual openings:** 39,000. **Job growth through 2012:** 13.0%.

7. Government and Public Administration

Managerial Work in Government and Public Administration

❑ **Top Executives**
Devise strategies and formulate policies to ensure that a business, corporation, nonprofit institution, government, or other organization meets its objectives. **Skill levels:** *High:* Communication, interpersonal, managerial, mathematics. *Moderate:* Science. *Basic:* Artistic. *Not essential:* Mechanical. **Education and training:** Work experience plus degree. **Annual earnings:** $88,922. **Annual openings:** 327,000. **Job growth through 2012:** 17.6%.

Public Planning

❑ **Urban and Regional Planners**
Develop comprehensive plans and programs for use of land and physical facilities of local jurisdictions, such as towns, cities, counties, and metropolitan areas. **Skill levels:** *High:* Mathematics. *Moderate:* Artistic, communication, interpersonal, managerial. *Basic:* Mechanical, science. **Education and training:** Master's degree. **Annual earnings:** $53,450. **Annual openings:** 5,000. **Job growth through 2012:** 10.7%.

Regulations Enforcement

❑ **Agricultural Workers**

Plant and harvest crops, install irrigation, deliver animals, and make sure that food is safe. **Skill levels:** *High:* Mechanical. *Basic:* Communication, interpersonal, managerial, mathematics, science. *Not essential:* Artistic. **Education and training:** Moderate-term on-the-job training. **Annual earnings:** $18,676. **Annual openings:** 40,000. **Job growth through 2012:** 6.2%.

❑ **Firefighting Occupations**

Control and extinguish fires or respond to emergency situations where life, property, or the environment is at risk. Duties may include fire prevention, emergency medical service, hazardous material response, search and rescue, and disaster management. **Skill levels:** *High:* Communication, mechanical. *Basic:* Interpersonal, managerial, mathematics, science. *Not essential:* Artistic. **Education and training:** Long-term on-the-job training. **Annual earnings:** $41,971. **Annual openings:** 7,178. **Job growth through 2012:** 20.0%.

❑ **Inspectors, Testers, Sorters, Samplers, and Weighers**

Inspect, test, sort, sample, or weigh nonagricultural raw materials or processed, machined, fabricated, or assembled parts or products for defects, wear, and deviations from specifications. **Skill levels:** *High:* Mechanical. *Moderate:* Communication, mathematics, science. *Basic:* Artistic, interpersonal. *Not essential:* Managerial. **Education and training:** Moderate-term on-the-job training. **Annual earnings:** $28,410. **Annual openings:** 87,000. **Job growth through 2012:** 4.7%.

❑ **Occupational Health and Safety Specialists and Technicians**

Help prevent harm to workers, property, and the environment as well as the general public. Promote occupational health and safety within organizations by developing safer, healthier, and more efficient ways of working. **Skill levels:** *Moderate:* Communication, managerial, mathematics, mechanical, science. *Basic:* Interpersonal. *Not essential:* Artistic. **Education and training:** Master's degree (does not apply to technicians). **Annual earnings:** $49,348. **Annual openings:** 6,000. **Job growth through 2012:** 13.2%.

❑ **Police and Detectives**

Maintain order, enforce laws and ordinances, and protect life and property in an assigned patrol district. May patrol a specific area on foot or in a vehicle; direct traffic; issue traffic summonses; investigate accidents and crimes; or make arrests. **Skill levels:** *High:* Communication, mechanical.

Moderate: Managerial. *Basic:* Interpersonal, mathematics, science. *Not essential:* Artistic. **Education and training:** Long-term on-the-job training. **Annual earnings:** $48,119. **Annual openings:** 83,000. **Job growth through 2012:** 23.0%.

❑ **Tax Examiners, Collectors, and Revenue Agents**
Ensure that governments obtain revenues from businesses and citizens by reviewing tax returns, conducting audits, identifying taxes payable, and collecting overdue tax dollars. **Skill levels:** *High:* Mathematics. *Basic:* Communication, interpersonal, managerial. *Not essential:* Artistic, mechanical, science. **Education and training:** Bachelor's degree. **Annual earnings:** $43,490. **Annual openings:** 9,000. **Job growth through 2012:** 5.0%.

Public Administration Clerical Support

❑ **Court Reporters**
Take verbatim reports of speeches, conversations, legal proceedings, meetings, and other events when written accounts of spoken words are necessary for correspondence, records, or legal proof. **Skill levels:** *High:* Mechanical. *Moderate:* Communication. *Basic:* Interpersonal. *Not essential:* Artistic, managerial, mathematics, science. **Education and training:** Postsecondary vocational award. **Annual earnings:** $42,920. **Annual openings:** 2,000. **Job growth through 2012:** 12.7%.

❑ **Information and Record Clerks**
Gather data and provide information to the public. Greet customers, guests, or other visitors. May answer telephones. **Skill levels:** *Moderate:* Communication, mathematics. *Basic:* Interpersonal. *Not essential:* Artistic, managerial, mechanical, science. **Education and training:** Moderate-term on-the-job training. **Annual earnings:** $26,402. **Annual openings:** 585,000. **Job growth through 2012:** 17.8%.

8. Health Science

Managerial Work in Medical and Health Services

❑ **Medical and Health Services Managers**
Plan, direct, coordinate, and supervise the delivery of health care. May be in charge of specific clinical departments or services or help to manage an entire facility or system. **Skill levels:** *High:* Communication, interpersonal,

managerial. *Moderate:* Mathematics, mechanical, science. *Not essential:* Artistic. **Education and training:** Work experience plus degree. **Annual earnings:** $67,430. **Annual openings:** 33,000. **Job growth through 2012:** 29.3%.

Medicine and Surgery

❑ **Medical Assistants**

Perform administrative and certain clinical duties under the direction of physician. Administrative duties may include scheduling appointments, maintaining medical records, billing, and coding for insurance purposes. **Skill levels:** *High:* Mechanical, science. *Moderate:* Communication, interpersonal, mathematics. *Basic:* Managerial. *Not essential:* Artistic. **Education and training:** Moderate-term on-the-job training. **Annual earnings:** $24,610. **Annual openings:** 78,000. **Job growth through 2012:** 58.9%.

❑ **Medical Transcriptionists**

Listen to dictated recordings made by physicians and other health care professionals and transcribe them into medical reports, correspondence, and other administrative material. **Skill levels:** *High:* Communication, science. *Basic:* Interpersonal, managerial, mathematics, mechanical. *Not essential:* Artistic. **Education and training:** Postsecondary vocational award. **Annual earnings:** $28,380. **Annual openings:** 18,000. **Job growth through 2012:** 22.6%.

❑ **Pharmacists**

Dispense drugs prescribed by physicians and other health practitioners and provide information to patients about medications and their use. **Skill levels:** *High:* Communication, mathematics, science. *Moderate:* Interpersonal, managerial. *Basic:* Mechanical. *Not essential:* Artistic. **Education and training:** First professional degree. **Annual earnings:** $84,900. **Annual openings:** 23,000. **Job growth through 2012:** 30.1%.

❑ **Pharmacy Aides**

Help licensed pharmacists with administrative duties in running a pharmacy, perhaps acting as clerks or cashiers who primarily answer telephones, handle money, stock shelves, and perform other clerical duties. Work closely with pharmacy technicians. **Skill levels:** *Moderate:* Communication, interpersonal. *Basic:* Managerial, mathematics, science. *Not essential:* Artistic, mechanical. **Education and training:** Short-term on-the-job training. **Annual earnings:** $18,420. **Annual openings:** 10,000. **Job growth through 2012:** 17.6%.

❏ **Pharmacy Technicians**
Prepare medications under the direction of a pharmacist. May measure, mix, count out, label, and record amounts and dosages of medications. **Skill levels:** *Moderate:* Communication, interpersonal, mathematics, mechanical, science. *Basic:* Managerial. *Not essential:* Artistic. **Education and training:** Moderate-term on-the-job training. **Annual earnings:** $23,650. **Annual openings:** 39,000. **Job growth through 2012:** 28.8%.

❏ **Physician Assistants**
Provide health care services typically performed by a physician, under the supervision of a physician. Conduct complete physicals, provide treatment, and counsel patients. May, in some cases, prescribe medication. **Skill levels:** *High:* Communication, interpersonal, mathematics, science. *Moderate:* Mechanical. *Basic:* Managerial. *Not essential:* Artistic. **Education and training:** Bachelor's degree. **Annual earnings:** $69,410. **Annual openings:** 7,000. **Job growth through 2012:** 48.9%.

❏ **Physicians and Surgeons**
Diagnose illnesses and prescribe and administer treatment for people suffering from injury or disease. May examine patients, obtain medical histories, and order, perform, and interpret diagnostic tests. **Skill levels:** *High:* Communication, interpersonal, managerial, mechanical, science. *Moderate:* Artistic, mathematics. **Education and training:** First professional degree. **Annual earnings:** more than $145,600. **Annual openings:** 38,000. **Job growth through 2012:** 19.5%.

❏ **Registered Nurses**
Assess patient health problems and needs, develop and implement nursing care plans, and maintain medical records. Administer nursing care to ill, injured, convalescent, or disabled patients. **Skill levels:** *High:* Communication, interpersonal, mathematics, mechanical, science. *Moderate:* Managerial. *Not essential:* Artistic. **Education and training:** Associate degree. **Annual earnings:** $52,330. **Annual openings:** 215,000. **Job growth through 2012:** 27.3%.

❏ **Surgical Technologists**
Assist in operations, under the supervision of surgeons, registered nurses, or other surgical personnel. **Skill levels:** *High:* Mathematics, mechanical, science. *Moderate:* Communication, interpersonal. *Basic:* Managerial. *Not essential:* Artistic. **Education and training:** Postsecondary vocational award. **Annual earnings:** $34,010. **Annual openings:** 13,000. **Job growth through 2012:** 27.9%.

Dentistry

❏ **Dental Assistants**

Assist dentist, set up patient and equipment, and keep records. **Skill levels:** *High:* Mechanical. *Moderate:* Communication, interpersonal, science. *Basic:* Managerial, mathematics. *Not essential:* Artistic. **Education and training:** Moderate-term on-the-job training. **Annual earnings:** $28,330. **Annual openings:** 35,000. **Job growth through 2012:** 42.5%.

❏ **Dental Hygienists**

Clean teeth and examine oral areas, head, and neck for signs of oral disease. May educate patients on oral hygiene, take and develop X rays, or apply fluoride or sealants. **Skill levels:** *High:* Mechanical. *Moderate:* Communication, interpersonal, mathematics, science. *Basic:* Managerial. *Not essential:* Artistic. **Education and training:** Associate degree. **Annual earnings:** $58,350. **Annual openings:** 9,000. **Job growth through 2012:** 43.1%.

❏ **Dentists**

Diagnose and treat diseases, injuries, and malformations of teeth and gums and related oral structures. May treat diseases of nerve, pulp, gums, and other dental tissues affecting vitality of teeth. **Skill levels:** *High:* Communication, interpersonal, managerial, mechanical, science. *Moderate:* Mathematics. *Basic:* Artistic. **Education and training:** First professional degree. **Annual earnings:** more than $145,600. **Annual openings:** 7,000. **Job growth through 2012:** 4.1%.

Health Specialties

❏ **Chiropractors**

Adjust spinal column and other articulations of the body to correct abnormalities of the human body believed to be caused by interference with the nervous system. Examine patient to determine nature and extent of disorder. **Skill levels:** *High:* Communication, managerial, science. *Moderate:* Interpersonal, mathematics. *Basic:* Mechanical. *Not essential:* Artistic. **Education and training:** First professional degree. **Annual earnings:** $69,910. **Annual openings:** 3,000. **Job growth through 2012:** 23.3%.

❏ **Optometrists**

Diagnose, manage, and treat conditions and diseases of the human eye and visual system. Examine eyes and visual system, diagnose problems or impairments, prescribe corrective lenses, and provide treatment. **Skill levels:** *High:* Communication, managerial, science. *Moderate:* Interpersonal, mathematics, mechanical. *Basic:* Artistic. **Education and training:** First professional degree. **Annual earnings:** $88,410. **Annual openings:** 2,000. **Job growth through 2012:** 17.1%.

❑ **Podiatrists**
Diagnose and treat diseases and deformities of the human foot. **Skill levels:** *High:* Communication, interpersonal, managerial, science. *Moderate:* Mathematics, mechanical. *Basic:* Artistic. **Education and training:** First professional degree. **Annual earnings:** $94,400. **Annual openings:** 1,000. **Job growth through 2012:** 15.0%.

Animal Care

❑ **Animal Care and Service Workers**
Train, feed, water, groom, bathe, and exercise animals, and clean, disinfect, and repair their cages. Play with the animals, provide companionship, and observe behavioral changes that could indicate illness or injury. **Skill levels:** *Moderate:* Mechanical. *Basic:* Communication, interpersonal, mathematics, science. *Not essential:* Artistic, managerial. **Education and training:** Short-term on-the-job training. **Annual earnings:** $18,250. **Annual openings:** 36,000. **Job growth through 2012:** 20.8%.

❑ **Veterinarians**
Diagnose and treat diseases and dysfunctions of animals. May engage in a particular function, such as research and development, consultation, administration, technical writing, sale or production of commercial products, or rendering of technical services. **Skill levels:** *High:* Communication, interpersonal, managerial, mathematics, mechanical, science. *Basic:* Artistic. **Education and training:** First professional degree. **Annual earnings:** $66,590. **Annual openings:** 4,000. **Job growth through 2012:** 25.1%.

❑ **Veterinary Technologists and Technicians**
Conduct clinical work in a private practice under the supervision of a veterinarian. May perform various medical tests, along with treating and diagnosing medical conditions and diseases in animals. **Skill levels:** *High:* Mechanical. *Moderate:* Communication, interpersonal, managerial, mathematics, science. *Not essential:* Artistic. **Education and training:** Associate degree. **Annual earnings:** $24,940. **Annual openings:** 11,000. **Job growth through 2012:** 44.1%.

Medical Technology

❑ **Cardiovascular Technologists and Technicians**
Conduct tests on pulmonary or cardiovascular systems of patients for diagnostic purposes. May conduct or assist in electrocardiograms, cardiac catheterizations, pulmonary-functions, lung capacity, and similar tests. **Skill levels:** *High:* Mathematics, mechanical, science. *Moderate:* Communication. *Basic:* Interpersonal, managerial. *Not essential:* Artistic. **Education and training:** Associate degree. **Annual earnings:** $38,690. **Annual openings:** 6,000. **Job growth through 2012:** 33.5%.

❑ **Clinical Laboratory Technologists and Technicians**
Perform medical laboratory tests for the diagnosis, treatment, and prevention of disease. Technologists may train or supervise staff. Technicians may work under the supervision of a medical technologist. **Skill levels:** *High:* Mathematics, mechanical, science. *Moderate:* Communication. *Basic:* Interpersonal, managerial. *Not essential:* Artistic. **Education and training:** Bachelor's degree. **Annual earnings:** $38,360. **Annual openings:** 42,000. **Job growth through 2012:** 19.3%.

❑ **Diagnostic Medical Sonographers**
Operate equipment that uses sound waves to generate an image for the assessment and diagnosis of various medical conditions. **Skill levels:** *High:* Mathematics, mechanical, science. *Moderate:* Communication. *Basic:* Interpersonal, managerial. *Not essential:* Artistic. **Education and training:** Associate degree. **Annual earnings:** $52,490. **Annual openings:** 4,000. **Job growth through 2012:** 24.0%.

❑ **Medical Records and Health Information Technicians**
Organize and evaluate health information records for completeness and accuracy. Communicate with physicians or other health care professionals to clarify diagnoses or to obtain additional information. **Skill levels:** *Moderate:* Communication, mathematics, science. *Basic:* Interpersonal, managerial. *Not essential:* Artistic, mechanical. **Education and training:** Associate degree. **Annual earnings:** $25,590. **Annual openings:** 24,000. **Job growth through 2012:** 46.8%.

❑ **Nuclear Medicine Technologists**
Prepare, administer, and measure radioactive isotopes in therapeutic, diagnostic, and tracer studies utilizing a variety of radioisotope equipment. **Skill levels:** *High:* Mathematics, mechanical, science. *Moderate:* Communication. *Basic:* Interpersonal, managerial. *Not essential:* Artistic. **Education and training:** Associate degree. **Annual earnings:** $56,450. **Annual openings:** 2,000. **Job growth through 2012:** 23.6%.

❑ **Opticians, Dispensing**
Design, measure, fit, and adapt lenses and frames for client according to written optical prescription or specification. Assist client with selecting frames. **Skill levels:** *Moderate:* Artistic, communication, interpersonal, mathematics, mechanical. *Basic:* Managerial, science. **Education and training:** Long-term on-the-job training. **Annual earnings:** $27,950. **Annual openings:** 10,000. **Job growth through 2012:** 18.2%.

❑ **Radiologic Technologists and Technicians**
Take X rays and CAT scans or administer nonradioactive materials into patient's blood stream for diagnostic purposes. May specialize in other modalities, such as computed tomography and magnetic resonance. **Skill levels:** *High:* Mathematics, mechanical. *Moderate:* Communication, interpersonal, science. *Basic:* Managerial. *Not essential:* Artistic. **Education and training:** Associate degree. **Annual earnings:** $43,350. **Annual openings:** 21,000. **Job growth through 2012:** 22.9%.

Medical Therapy

❑ **Audiologists**
Assess and treat persons with hearing and related disorders. May fit hearing aids and provide auditory training. May perform research related to hearing problems. **Skill levels:** *High:* Communication, managerial, science. *Moderate:* Interpersonal, mathematics. *Basic:* Mechanical. *Not essential:* Artistic. **Education and training:** Master's degree. **Annual earnings:** $51,470. **Annual openings:** 1,000. **Job growth through 2012:** 29.0%.

❑ **Occupational Therapist Assistants and Aides**
Assist occupational therapists in providing occupational therapy treatments and procedures. **Skill levels:** *High:* Interpersonal, mechanical. *Moderate:* Communication, science. *Basic:* Managerial, mathematics. *Not essential:* Artistic. **Education and training:** Associate degree (does not apply to aides). **Annual earnings:** $33,728. **Annual openings:** 4,000. **Job growth through 2012:** 40.2%.

❑ **Occupational Therapists**
Assess, plan, organize, and participate in rehabilitative programs that help restore vocational, homemaking, and daily living skills, as well as general independence, to disabled persons. **Skill levels:** *High:* Communication, interpersonal. *Moderate:* Managerial, mathematics, mechanical, science. *Not essential:* Artistic. **Education and training:** Bachelor's degree. **Annual earnings:** $54,660. **Annual openings:** 10,000. **Job growth through 2012:** 35.2%.

❑ **Physical Therapist Assistants and Aides**
Perform components of physical therapy procedures and related tasks selected by a supervising physical therapist. **Skill levels:** *Moderate:* Communication, interpersonal, mechanical, science. *Basic:* Managerial, mathematics. *Not essential:* Artistic. **Education and training:** Associate degree. **Annual earnings:** $30,869. **Annual openings:** 18,000. **Job growth through 2012:** 45.4%.

❑ **Physical Therapists**
Assess, plan, organize, and participate in rehabilitative programs that improve mobility, relieve pain, increase strength, and decrease or prevent deformity of patients suffering from disease or injury. **Skill levels:** *High:* Communication, interpersonal, science. *Moderate:* Mathematics. *Basic:* Managerial, mechanical. *Not essential:* Artistic. **Education and training:** Master's degree. **Annual earnings:** $60,180. **Annual openings:** 16,000. **Job growth through 2012:** 35.3%.

❑ **Recreational Therapists**
Plan, direct, or coordinate medically approved recreation programs for patients in hospitals, nursing homes, or other institutions. Activities include sports, trips, dramatics, social activities, and arts and crafts. **Skill levels:** *High:* Artistic, communication, interpersonal. *Basic:* Managerial, mathematics, mechanical, science. **Education and training:** Bachelor's degree. **Annual earnings:** $32,900. **Annual openings:** 3,000. **Job growth through 2012:** 9.1%.

❑ **Respiratory Therapists**
Assess, treat, and care for patients with breathing disorders. Assume primary responsibility for all respiratory care modalities, including the supervision of respiratory therapy technicians. **Skill levels:** *High:* Communication, interpersonal, mathematics, mechanical, science. *Basic:* Managerial. *Not essential:* Artistic. **Education and training:** Associate degree. **Annual earnings:** $43,140. **Annual openings:** 10,000. **Job growth through 2012:** 34.8%.

❑ **Speech-Language Pathologists**
Assess and treat persons with speech, language, voice, and fluency disorders. May select alternative communication systems and teach their use. May perform research related to speech and language problems. **Skill levels:** *High:* Communication, interpersonal, mathematics, science. *Basic:* Artistic, managerial, mechanical. **Education and training:** Master's degree. **Annual earnings:** $52,410. **Annual openings:** 10,000. **Job growth through 2012:** 27.2%.

Patient Care and Assistance

❑ **Licensed Practical and Licensed Vocational Nurses**

Care for ill, injured, convalescent, or disabled persons in hospitals, nursing homes, clinics, private homes, group homes, and similar institutions. May work under the supervision of a registered nurse. Licensing required. **Skill levels:** *High:* Interpersonal, mechanical, science. *Moderate:* Communication. *Basic:* Managerial, mathematics. *Not essential:* Artistic. **Education and training:** Postsecondary vocational award. **Annual earnings:** $33,970. **Annual openings:** 105,000. **Job growth through 2012:** 20.2%.

❑ **Nursing, Psychiatric, and Home Health Aides**

Help care for physically or mentally ill, injured, disabled, or infirm individuals at home or in hospitals, nursing care facilities, or mental health settings. **Skill levels:** *Moderate:* Communication, interpersonal, mechanical. *Basic:* Managerial, mathematics, science. *Not essential:* Artistic. **Education and training:** Short-term on-the-job training. **Annual earnings:** $20,284. **Annual openings:** 455,000. **Job growth through 2012:** 31.3%.

Health Protection and Promotion

❑ **Dietitians and Nutritionists**

Plan and conduct food service or nutritional programs to assist in the promotion of health and control of disease. May supervise activities of a department providing quantity food services, counsel individuals, or conduct nutritional research. **Skill levels:** *High:* Communication, interpersonal, science. *Moderate:* Mathematics. *Basic:* Managerial, mechanical. *Not essential:* Artistic. **Education and training:** Bachelor's degree. **Annual earnings:** $43,630. **Annual openings:** 8,000. **Job growth through 2012:** 17.8%.

9. Hospitality, Tourism, and Recreation

Managerial Work in Hospitality and Tourism

❑ **Food Service Managers**

Oversee the daily operations of restaurants and other establishments that prepare and serve meals and beverages to customers. **Skill levels:** *High:* Communication, interpersonal, managerial. *Moderate:* Artistic, mathematics, mechanical. *Basic:* Science. **Education and training:** Work experience in a related occupation. **Annual earnings:** $39,610. **Annual openings:** 58,000. **Job growth through 2012:** 11.5%.

❑ **Lodging Managers**

Keep a hotel, motel, or other lodging facility efficient and profitable. Oversee all aspects of operations or specialize. For business travelers, may schedule available meeting rooms and electronic equipment. **Skill levels:** *High:* Communication, interpersonal, managerial. *Moderate:* Mathematics. *Basic:* Artistic, mechanical. *Not essential:* Science. **Education and training:** Work experience in a related occupation. **Annual earnings:** $37,660. **Annual openings:** 10,000. **Job growth through 2012:** 6.6%.

Recreational Services

❑ **Gaming Services Occupations**

Perform supervision, surveillance, and investigation of gaming establishments, or work with the games or patrons themselves, performing such activities as tending slot machines, handling money, and dealing cards. **Skill levels:** *High:* Interpersonal, managerial. *Moderate:* Communication. *Basic:* Artistic, mathematics, mechanical. *Not essential:* Science. **Education and training:** Postsecondary vocational award. **Annual earnings:** $14,956. **Annual openings:** 31,000. **Job growth through 2012:** 24.7%.

❑ **Recreation and Fitness Workers**

Conduct recreation activities with groups in public, private, or volunteer agencies or recreation facilities. Organize and promote activities, such as arts and crafts, sports, games, music, dramatics, social recreation, camping, and hobbies. **Skill levels:** *High:* Communication, interpersonal. *Basic:* Artistic, managerial, mathematics, mechanical, science. **Education and training:** Bachelor's degree. **Annual earnings:** $21,641. **Annual openings:** 94,000. **Job growth through 2012:** 29.6%.

Hospitality and Travel Services

❑ **Building Cleaning Workers**

Keep office buildings, hospitals, stores, apartment houses, hotels, and residences clean and in good condition. **Skill levels:** *High:* Mechanical. *Basic:* Artistic, communication, mathematics. *Not essential:* Interpersonal, managerial, science. **Education and training:** Short-term on-the-job training. **Annual earnings:** $18,040. **Annual openings:** 806,000. **Job growth through 2012:** 14.7%.

❑ **Flight Attendants**

Provide personal services to ensure the safety and comfort of airline passengers during flight. Greet passengers, verify tickets, explain use of safety equipment, and serve food or beverages. **Skill levels:** *High:* Communication, interpersonal. *Basic:* Managerial, mathematics, mechanical. *Not essential:* Artistic, science. **Education and training:** Long-term on-the-job training. **Annual earnings:** $43,440. **Annual openings:** 23,000. **Job growth through 2012:** 15.9%.

❑ **Hotel, Motel, and Resort Desk Clerks**

Accommodate hotel, motel, and resort patrons by registering and assigning rooms to guests, issuing room keys, transmitting and receiving messages, keeping records of occupied rooms and guests' accounts, and making and confirming reservations. **Skill levels:** *High:* Interpersonal. *Moderate:* Communication. *Basic:* Artistic, managerial, mathematics. *Not essential:* Mechanical, science. **Education and training:** Short-term on-the-job training. **Annual earnings:** $17,700. **Annual openings:** 46,000. **Job growth through 2012:** 23.9%.

❑ **Information and Record Clerks**

Gather data and provide information to the public. Greet customers, guests, or other visitors. May answer telephones. **Skill levels:** *Moderate:* Communication, mathematics. *Basic:* Interpersonal. *Not essential:* Artistic, managerial, mechanical, science. **Education and training:** Moderate-term on-the-job training. **Annual earnings:** $26,402. **Annual openings:** 585,000. **Job growth through 2012:** 17.8%.

❑ **Reservation and Transportation Ticket Agents and Travel Clerks**

Make and confirm reservations and sell tickets to passengers for large hotel or motel chains. **Skill levels:** *High:* Interpersonal. *Moderate:* Mathematics. *Basic:* Communication. *Not essential:* Artistic, managerial, mechanical, science. **Education and training:** Short-term on-the-job training. **Annual earnings:** $27,750. **Annual openings:** 35,000. **Job growth through 2012:** 12.2%.

❑ **Travel Agents**

Plan and sell transportation and accommodations for travel agency customers. Determine destination, modes of transportation, travel dates, costs, and accommodations required. **Skill levels:** *High:* Interpersonal. *Moderate:* Communication. *Basic:* Mathematics. *Not essential:* Artistic, managerial, mechanical, science. **Education and training:** Postsecondary vocational award. **Annual earnings:** $27,640. **Annual openings:** 14,000. **Job growth through 2012:** –13.8%.

Food and Beverage Preparation

❑ **Chefs, Cooks, and Food Preparation Workers**

Prepare, season, and cook soups, meats, vegetables, desserts, baked goods, or other foodstuffs in restaurants. May order supplies, keep records and accounts, price items on menu, or plan menu. **Skill levels:** *High:* Artistic, managerial. *Moderate:* Communication, interpersonal, mechanical. *Basic:* Mathematics, science. **Education and training:** Short-term on-the-job training. **Annual earnings:** $17,967. **Annual openings:** 863,000. **Job growth through 2012:** 12.3%.

❑ **Food Processing Occupations**

Process raw food products into the finished goods sold by grocers or wholesalers, restaurants, or institutional food services. May work with meats, baked goods, or other foods that are prepared in batches. **Skill levels:** *High:* Mechanical. *Basic:* Communication, mathematics. *Not essential:* Artistic, interpersonal, managerial, science. **Education and training:** Moderate-term on-the-job training. **Annual earnings:** $21,687. **Annual openings:** 119,000. **Job growth through 2012:** 10.3%.

Food and Beverage Service

❑ **Food and Beverage Serving and Related Workers**

Greet customers, escort them to seats and hand them menus, take food and drink orders, and serve food and beverages. Answer questions, explain menu items and specials, and keep tables and dining areas clean and set for new diners. **Skill levels:** *High:* Interpersonal. *Moderate:* Communication. *Basic:* Artistic, mathematics. *Not essential:* Managerial, mechanical, science. **Education and training:** Short-term on-the-job training. **Annual earnings:** $14,701. **Annual openings:** 2,149,000. **Job growth through 2012:** 17.6%.

Sports

❑ **Athletes, Coaches, Umpires, and Related Workers**

Compete in organized, officiated sports events to entertain spectators; organize, instruct, and teach amateur and professional athletes either individually or as teams; officiate at competitive sporting events; or evaluate the skills of athletes. **Skill levels:** *High:* Managerial. *Moderate:* Artistic, communication, interpersonal. *Basic:* Mechanical, science. *Not essential:* Mathematics. **Education and training:** Long-term on-the-job training. **Annual earnings:** $27,974. **Annual openings:** 32,000. **Job growth through 2012:** 18.3%.

Barber and Beauty Services

❑ **Barbers, Cosmetologists, and Other Personal Appearance Workers**
Help people look neat and well-groomed by providing services such as shampooing, cutting, coloring, and styling hair, and massaging and treating scalp. May provide nail and skin care services or apply makeup to performers. **Skill levels:** *High:* Artistic. *Moderate:* Communication, mechanical. *Basic:* Interpersonal, mathematics, science. *Not essential:* Managerial. **Education and training:** Postsecondary vocational award. **Annual earnings:** $19,814. **Annual openings:** 88,000. **Job growth through 2012:** 14.8%.

10. Human Service

Counseling and Social Work

❑ **Counselors**
Counsel individuals and provide group educational and vocational guidance services. Assist people with personal, family, educational, mental health, and career decisions and problems. **Skill levels:** *High:* Communication, interpersonal. *Basic:* Managerial, mathematics, science. *Not essential:* Artistic, mechanical. **Education and training:** Master's degree. **Annual earnings:** $37,411. **Annual openings:** 77,000. **Job growth through 2012:** 22.6%.

❑ **Probation Officers and Correctional Treatment Specialists**
Supervise people who have been placed on probation, or counsel prison inmates and help them plan for their release from incarceration. **Skill levels:** *Moderate:* Communication, interpersonal. *Basic:* Managerial, mathematics, mechanical, science. *Not essential:* Artistic. **Education and training:** Bachelor's degree. **Annual earnings:** $39,600. **Annual openings:** 15,000. **Job growth through 2012:** 14.7%.

❑ **Psychologists**
Study the human mind and human behavior. In research, investigate the physical, cognitive, emotional, or social aspects of human behavior. In health service provider fields, provide mental health care in hospitals, clinics, schools, or private settings. **Skill levels:** *High:* Communication, interpersonal. *Moderate:* Mathematics, science. *Basic:* Managerial. *Not essential:* Artistic, mechanical. **Education and training:** Doctoral degree. **Annual earnings:** $55,187. **Annual openings:** 17,000. **Job growth through 2012:** 24.3%.

❏ **Social and Human Service Assistants**

Provide direct and indirect client services to ensure that individuals reach their maximum level of functioning. **Skill levels:** *High:* Interpersonal. *Moderate:* Communication. *Basic:* Science. *Not essential:* Artistic, managerial, mathematics, mechanical. **Education and training:** Moderate-term on-the-job training. **Annual earnings:** $24,270. **Annual openings:** 63,000. **Job growth through 2012:** 48.7%.

❏ **Social Workers**

Help people function the best way they can in their environment, deal with their relationships, and solve personal and family problems. **Skill levels:** *High:* Communication, interpersonal. *Basic:* Managerial, mathematics, science. *Not essential:* Artistic, mechanical. **Education and training:** Bachelor's degree (master's degree required in many positions). **Annual earnings:** $35,823. **Annual openings:** 80,000. **Job growth through 2012:** 26.7%.

Religious Work

❏ **Clergy**

Conduct religious worship and perform other spiritual functions associated with beliefs and practices of religious faith or denomination. Provide spiritual and moral guidance and assistance to members. **Skill levels:** *High:* Communication, interpersonal, managerial. *Basic:* Artistic, mathematics. *Not essential:* Mechanical, science. **Education and training:** First professional degree. **Annual earnings:** $36,690. **Annual openings:** 34,000. **Job growth through 2012:** 15.5%.

Child/Personal Care and Services

❏ **Childcare Workers**

Nurture and teach children of all ages in childcare centers, nursery schools, preschools, public schools, private households, family childcare homes, and before- and after-school programs. **Skill levels:** *High:* Interpersonal. *Moderate:* Communication. *Basic:* Artistic, managerial, mathematics, mechanical. *Not essential:* Science. **Education and training:** Short-term on-the-job training. **Annual earnings:** $16,760. **Annual openings:** 406,000. **Job growth through 2012:** 11.7%.

❏ **Personal and Home Care Aides**

Help elderly, disabled, and ill persons live in their own homes or in residential care facilities instead of in a health facility. **Skill levels:** *High:*

Interpersonal. *Moderate:* Communication. *Basic:* Managerial, mathematics, science. *Not essential:* Artistic, mechanical. **Education and training:** Short-term on-the-job training. **Annual earnings:** $16,900. **Annual openings:** 154,000. **Job growth through 2012:** 40.5%.

Client Interviewing

❑ **Information and Record Clerks**
Gather data and provide information to the public. Greet customers, guests, or other visitors. May answer telephones. **Skill levels:** *Moderate:* Communication, mathematics. *Basic:* Interpersonal. *Not essential:* Artistic, managerial, mechanical, science. **Education and training:** Moderate-term on-the-job training. **Annual earnings:** $26,402. **Annual openings:** 585,000. **Job growth through 2012:** 17.8%.

❑ **Interviewers**
Interview persons by telephone, mail, in person, or by other means for the purpose of completing forms, applications, or questionnaires. Ask specific questions, record answers, and assist persons with completing form. May sort, classify, and file forms. **Skill levels:** *High:* Communication. *Moderate:* Interpersonal, managerial. *Basic:* Mathematics, science. *Not essential:* Artistic, mechanical. **Education and training:** Short-term on-the-job training. **Annual earnings:** $27,594. **Annual openings:** 1,883. **Job growth through 2012:** 4.1%.

11. Information Technology

Managerial Work in Information Technology

❑ **Computer and Information Systems Managers**
Plan, coordinate, and direct research and design of the computer-related activities of firms. Help determine both technical and business goals in consultation with top management, and make detailed plans for the accomplishment of these goals. **Skill levels:** *High:* Communication, interpersonal, managerial, mathematics, mechanical, science. *Not essential:* Artistic. **Education and training:** Work experience plus degree. **Annual earnings:** $92,570. **Annual openings:** 39,000. **Job growth through 2012:** 36.1%.

❑ **Computer Support Specialists and Systems Administrators**
Provide technical assistance, support, and advice to customers and other users of computer systems and networks. Also provide day-to-day administration, maintenance, and support. **Skill levels:** *High:* Mechanical.

Moderate: Communication, interpersonal, mathematics, science. *Basic:* Managerial. *Not essential:* Artistic. **Education and training:** Associate degree. **Annual earnings:** $46,311. **Annual openings:** 106,000. **Job growth through 2012:** 32.7%.

Information Technology Specialties

❑ **Computer Operators**

Monitor and control electronic computer and peripheral electronic data processing equipment to process business, scientific, engineering, and other data according to operating instructions. **Skill levels:** *Moderate:* Mechanical. *Basic:* Communication, mathematics, science. *Not essential:* Artistic, interpersonal, managerial. **Education and training:** Moderate-term on-the-job training. **Annual earnings:** $31,070. **Annual openings:** 27,000. **Job growth through 2012:** –16.7%.

❑ **Computer Programmers**

Convert project specifications and statements of problems and procedures to detailed logical flow charts for coding into computer language. Develop and write computer programs to store, locate, and retrieve specific documents, data, and information. **Skill levels:** *High:* Mathematics, science. *Moderate:* Communication, mechanical. *Basic:* Interpersonal, managerial. *Not essential:* Artistic. **Education and training:** Bachelor's degree. **Annual earnings:** $62,890. **Annual openings:** 45,000. **Job growth through 2012:** 14.6%.

❑ **Computer Software Engineers**

Research, design, develop, and test software. Analyze user needs and develop software solutions, applying principles and techniques of computer science, engineering, and mathematical analysis. **Skill levels:** *High:* Mathematics, mechanical, science. *Moderate:* Communication, interpersonal, managerial. *Not essential:* Artistic. **Education and training:** Bachelor's degree. **Annual earnings:** $76,962. **Annual openings:** 94,000. **Job growth through 2012:** 45.5%.

❑ **Computer Support Specialists and Systems Administrators**

Provide technical assistance, support, and advice to customers and other users of computer systems and networks. Also provide day-to-day administration, maintenance, and support. **Skill levels:** *High:* Mechanical. *Moderate:* Communication, interpersonal, mathematics, science. *Basic:* Managerial. *Not essential:* Artistic. **Education and training:** Associate degree. **Annual earnings:** $46,311. **Annual openings:** 106,000. **Job growth through 2012:** 32.7%.

❑ **Computer Systems Analysts, Database Administrators, and Computer Scientists**
Solve computer problems and apply computer technology to meet the individual needs of an organization, or work with database management systems software and determine ways to organize and store data. **Skill levels:** *High:* Mathematics, science. *Moderate:* Communication. *Basic:* Interpersonal, managerial. *Not essential:* Artistic, mechanical. **Education and training:** Bachelor's degree. **Annual earnings:** $64,197. **Annual openings:** 113,000. **Job growth through 2012:** 44.4%.

Digital Equipment Repair

❑ **Coin and Vending, and Amusement Machine Servicers and Repairers**
Install, service, adjust, or repair coin, vending, or amusement machines, including video games, jukeboxes, pinball machines, or slot machines. **Skill levels:** *High:* Mechanical. *Basic:* Communication, mathematics. *Not essential:* Artistic, interpersonal, managerial, science. **Education and training:** Moderate-term on-the-job training. **Annual earnings:** $28,010. **Annual openings:** 7,000. **Job growth through 2012:** 15.2%.

❑ **Computer, Automated Teller, and Office Machine Repairers**
Repair, maintain, or install computers, word processing systems, automated teller machines, and electronic office machines, such as duplicating and fax machines. **Skill levels:** *High:* Mechanical. *Basic:* Communication, interpersonal, mathematics, science. *Not essential:* Artistic, managerial. **Education and training:** Postsecondary vocational award. **Annual earnings:** $35,150. **Annual openings:** 19,000. **Job growth through 2012:** 15.1%.

12. Law and Public Safety

Managerial Work in Law and Public Safety

❑ Firefighting Occupations
Control and extinguish fires or respond to emergency situations where life, property, or the environment is at risk. Duties may include fire prevention, emergency medical service, hazardous material response, search and rescue, and disaster management. **Skill levels:** *High:* Communication, mechanical. *Basic:* Interpersonal, managerial, mathematics, science. *Not essential:* Artistic. **Education and training:** Long-term on-the-job training. **Annual earnings:** $41,971. **Annual openings:** 7,178. **Job growth through 2012:** 20.0%.

❏ **Police and Detectives**

Maintain order, enforce laws and ordinances, and protect life and property in an assigned patrol district. May patrol a specific area on foot or in a vehicle, direct traffic, issue traffic summonses, investigate accidents and crimes, or make arrests. **Skill levels:** *High:* Communication, mechanical. *Moderate:* Managerial. *Basic:* Interpersonal, mathematics, science. *Not essential:* Artistic. **Education and training:** Long-term on-the-job training. **Annual earnings:** $48,119. **Annual openings:** 83,000. **Job growth through 2012:** 23.0%.

Legal Practice and Justice Administration

❏ **Judges, Magistrates, and Other Judicial Workers**

Arbitrate, advise, adjudicate, or administer justice in a court of law. May sentence defendant in criminal cases according to government statutes. May determine liability of defendant in civil cases. May issue marriage licenses and perform weddings. **Skill levels:** *High:* Communication. *Basic:* Interpersonal, managerial, mathematics, science. *Not essential:* Artistic, mechanical. **Education and training:** Work experience plus degree. **Annual earnings:** $79,829. **Annual openings:** 427. **Job growth through 2012:** 8.2%.

❏ **Lawyers**

Represent clients in criminal and civil litigation and other legal proceedings, draw up legal documents, and manage or advise clients on legal transactions. May specialize in a single area or may practice broadly in many areas of law. **Skill levels:** *High:* Communication, interpersonal, managerial. *Basic:* Mathematics, science. *Not essential:* Artistic, mechanical. **Education and training:** First professional degree. **Annual earnings:** $94,930. **Annual openings:** 53,000. **Job growth through 2012:** 17.0%.

Legal Support

❏ **Paralegals and Legal Assistants**

Assist lawyers by researching legal precedent, investigating facts, or preparing legal documents. Conduct research to support a legal proceeding, to formulate a defense, or to initiate legal action. **Skill levels:** *High:* Communication, interpersonal. *Basic:* Managerial, mathematics, science. *Not essential:* Artistic, mechanical. **Education and training:** Associate degree. **Annual earnings:** $39,130. **Annual openings:** 29,000. **Job growth through 2012:** 28.7%.

Law Enforcement and Public Safety

❑ **Correctional Officers**

Guard inmates in penal or rehabilitative institution in accordance with established regulations and procedures. May guard prisoners in transit between jail, courtroom, prison, or other point. **Skill levels:** *Moderate:* Communication. *Basic:* Interpersonal, managerial, mathematics, mechanical. *Not essential:* Artistic, science. **Education and training:** Moderate-term on-the-job training. **Annual earnings:** $33,600. **Annual openings:** 49,000. **Job growth through 2012:** 24.2%.

❑ **Police and Detectives**

Maintain order, enforce laws and ordinances, and protect life and property in an assigned patrol district. May patrol a specific area on foot or in a vehicle, direct traffic, issue traffic summonses, investigate accidents and crimes, or make arrests. **Skill levels:** *High:* Communication, mechanical. *Moderate:* Managerial. *Basic:* Interpersonal, mathematics, science. *Not essential:* Artistic. **Education and training:** Long-term on-the-job training. **Annual earnings:** $48,119. **Annual openings:** 83,000. **Job growth through 2012:** 23.0%.

Safety and Security

❑ **Private Detectives and Investigators**

Detect occurrences of unlawful acts or infractions of rules in private establishment, or seek, examine, and compile information for client. **Skill levels:** *High:* Communication, mechanical. *Moderate:* Managerial. *Basic:* Interpersonal, mathematics, science. *Not essential:* Artistic. **Education and training:** Work experience in a related occupation. **Annual earnings:** $32,110. **Annual openings:** 9,000. **Job growth through 2012:** 25.3%.

❑ **Security Guards and Gaming Surveillance Officers**

Patrol and inspect property or vehicle transporting valuables to protect against fire, theft, vandalism, terrorism, and illegal activity. May specialize in monitoring casino operations. **Skill levels:** *Basic:* Communication, interpersonal, managerial, mechanical. *Not essential:* Artistic, mathematics, science. **Education and training:** Short-term on-the-job training. **Annual earnings:** $20,369. **Annual openings:** 230,000. **Job growth through 2012:** 31.8%.

Emergency Responding

❑ **Emergency Medical Technicians and Paramedics**

Assess injuries, administer emergency medical care, and extricate trapped individuals. Transport injured or sick persons to medical facilities. **Skill levels:** *High:* Communication, interpersonal, managerial, mechanical, science. *Basic:* Mathematics. *Not essential:* Artistic. **Education and training:** Postsecondary vocational award. **Annual earnings:** $25,310. **Annual openings:** 32,000. **Job growth through 2012:** 33.1%.

❑ **Firefighting Occupations**
Control and extinguish fires or respond to emergency situations where life, property, or the environment is at risk. Duties may include fire prevention, emergency medical service, hazardous material response, search and rescue, and disaster management. **Skill levels:** *High:* Communication, mechanical. *Basic:* Interpersonal, managerial, mathematics, science. *Not essential:* Artistic. **Education and training:** Long-term on-the-job training. **Annual earnings:** $41,971. **Annual openings:** 7,178. **Job growth through 2012:** 20.0%.

13. Manufacturing

Managerial Work in Manufacturing

❑ **Industrial Production Managers**
Plan, direct, or coordinate the work activities and resources necessary for manufacturing products in accordance with cost, quality, and quantity specifications. **Skill levels:** *High:* Communication, interpersonal, managerial, mathematics. *Moderate:* Science. *Basic:* Mechanical. *Not essential:* Artistic. **Education and training:** Bachelor's degree. **Annual earnings:** $73,000. **Annual openings:** 18,000. **Job growth through 2012:** 7.9%.

Machine Setup and Operation

❑ **Bookbinders and Bindery Workers**
Set up or operate binding machines that produce books and other printed materials, or perform highly skilled hand finishing operations, such as grooving and lettering, to bind books. **Skill levels:** *High:* Mechanical. *Basic:* Artistic, communication, mathematics, science. *Not essential:* Interpersonal, managerial. **Education and training:** Moderate-term on-the-job training. **Annual earnings:** $23,878. **Annual openings:** 6,000. **Job growth through 2012:** –4.7%.

❑ **Machine Setters, Operators, and Tenders—Metal and Plastic**
Prepare industrial machines prior to production and adjust the machinery during its operation. **Skill levels:** *High:* Mathematics, mechanical.

Moderate: Science. *Basic:* Communication. *Not essential:* Artistic, inter-personal, managerial. **Education and training:** Moderate-term on-the-job training. **Annual earnings:** $27,717. **Annual openings:** 127,000. **Job growth through 2012:** 4.9%.

❑ **Painting and Coating Workers, Except Construction and Maintenance**
Control the machinery that applies paints and coatings to a wide range of manufactured products. May dip an item in a large vat of paint or other coating or spray products with a solution of paint or some other coating. **Skill levels:** *High:* Mechanical. *Basic:* Artistic, communication, mathematics. *Not essential:* Interpersonal, managerial, science. **Education and training:** Moderate-term on-the-job training. **Annual earnings:** $28,016. **Annual openings:** 32,000. **Job growth through 2012:** 13.1%.

❑ **Printing Machine Operators**
Set up or operate various types of printing machines, such as offset, letter-set, intaglio, or gravure presses or screen printers to produce print on paper or other materials. **Skill levels:** *High:* Mechanical. *Basic:* Communication, mathematics, science. *Not essential:* Artistic, interpersonal, managerial. **Education and training:** Moderate-term on-the-job training. **Annual earnings:** $29,900. **Annual openings:** 30,000. **Job growth through 2012:** 4.6%.

❑ **Textile, Apparel, and Furnishings Occupations**
Produce textile and leather materials and fashion them into a wide range of garment and nongarment products. May operate large industrial machin-ery, smaller power equipment, or do substantial handwork. **Skill levels:** *High:* Mechanical. *Moderate:* Artistic. *Basic:* Communication, mathematics. *Not essential:* Interpersonal, managerial, science. **Education and training:** Moderate-term on-the-job training. **Annual earnings:** $19,619. **Annual openings:** 161,000. **Job growth through 2012:** –15.1%.

❑ **Welding, Soldering, and Brazing Workers**
Apply heat to metal pieces, melting and fusing them to form a permanent bond. May control all the work manually or use machinery, such as a wire feeder. **Skill levels:** *High:* Mechanical. *Basic:* Artistic, communication, mathematics, science. *Not essential:* Interpersonal, managerial. **Education and training:** Long-term on-the-job training. **Annual earnings:** $16,190. **Annual openings:** 4,000. **Job growth through 2012:** 1.1%.

❑ **Woodworkers**

Play a role in processing wood into finished products. May produce structural elements of buildings; mill hardwood and softwood lumber; assemble finished wood products; or operate machines that cut, shape, assemble, and finish raw wood. **Skill levels:** *High:* Mechanical. *Moderate:* Artistic, mathematics. *Basic:* Communication, science. *Not essential:* Interpersonal, managerial. **Education and training:** Long-term on-the-job training. **Annual earnings:** $24,062. **Annual openings:** 42,000. **Job growth through 2012:** 5.4%.

Production Work, Assorted Materials Processing

❑ **Assemblers and Fabricators**

Produce a wide range of finished goods, such as aircraft, automobile engines, computers, and electrical and electronic components, from manufactured parts or subassemblies. **Skill levels:** *High:* Mechanical. *Basic:* Artistic, communication, mathematics, science. *Not essential:* Interpersonal, managerial. **Education and training:** Moderate-term on-the-job training. **Annual earnings:** $24,840. **Annual openings:** 193,000. **Job growth through 2012:** –4.3%.

❑ **Food Processing Occupations**

Process raw food products into the finished goods sold by grocers or wholesalers, restaurants, or institutional food services. May work with meats, baked goods, or other foods that are prepared in batches. **Skill levels:** *High:* Mechanical. *Basic:* Communication, mathematics. *Not essential:* Artistic, interpersonal, managerial, science. **Education and training:** Moderate-term on-the-job training. **Annual earnings:** $21,687. **Annual openings:** 119,000. **Job growth through 2012:** 10.3%.

❑ **Machine Setters, Operators, and Tenders—Metal and Plastic**

Prepare industrial machines prior to production and adjust the machinery during its operation. **Skill levels:** *High:* Mathematics, mechanical. *Moderate:* Science. *Basic:* Communication. *Not essential:* Artistic, interpersonal, managerial. **Education and training:** Moderate-term on-the-job training. **Annual earnings:** $27,717. **Annual openings:** 127,000. **Job growth through 2012:** 4.9%.

❑ **Textile, Apparel, and Furnishings Occupations**

Produce textile and leather materials and fashion them into a wide range of garment and nongarment products. May operate large industrial machinery, smaller power equipment, or do substantial handwork. **Skill levels:** *High:* Mechanical. *Moderate:* Artistic. *Basic:* Communication, mathematics.

Not essential: Interpersonal, managerial, science. **Education and training:** Moderate-term on-the-job training. **Annual earnings:** $19,619. **Annual openings:** 161,000. **Job growth through 2012:** –15.1%.

❏ **Woodworkers**
Play a role in processing wood into finished products. May produce structural elements of buildings; mill hardwood and softwood lumber; assemble finished wood products; or operate machines that cut, shape, assemble, and finish raw wood. **Skill levels:** *High:* Mechanical. *Moderate:* Artistic, mathematics. *Basic:* Communication, science. *Not essential:* Interpersonal, managerial. **Education and training:** Long-term on-the-job training. **Annual earnings:** $24,062. **Annual openings:** 42,000. **Job growth through 2012:** 5.4%.

Welding, Brazing, and Soldering

❏ **Assemblers and Fabricators**
Produce a wide range of finished goods, such as aircraft, automobile engines, computers, and electrical and electronic components, from manufactured parts or subassemblies. **Skill levels:** *High:* Mechanical. *Basic:* Artistic, communication, mathematics, science. *Not essential:* Interpersonal, managerial. **Education and training:** Moderate-term on-the-job training. **Annual earnings:** $24,840. **Annual openings:** 193,000. **Job growth through 2012:** –4.3%.

❏ **Welding, Soldering, and Brazing Workers**
Apply heat to metal pieces, melting and fusing them to form a permanent bond. May control all the work manually or use machinery, such as a wire feeder. **Skill levels:** *High:* Mechanical. *Basic:* Artistic, communication, mathematics, science. *Not essential:* Interpersonal, managerial. **Education and training:** Long-term on-the-job training. **Annual earnings:** $16,190. **Annual openings:** 4,000. **Job growth through 2012:** 1.1%.

Production Machining Technology

❏ **Computer Control Programmers and Operators**
Use computer numerically controlled (CNC) machines to cut and shape precision products, such as automobile parts, machine parts, and compressors. **Skill levels:** *Moderate:* Mathematics, mechanical. *Basic:* Communication, science. *Not essential:* Artistic, interpersonal, managerial. **Education and training:** Moderate-term on-the-job training. **Annual earnings:** $31,883. **Annual openings:** 13,000. **Job growth through 2012:** 9.8%.

❑ **Machine Setters, Operators, and Tenders—Metal and Plastic**
Prepare industrial machines prior to production and adjust the machinery during its operation. **Skill levels:** _High:_ Mathematics, mechanical. _Moderate:_ Science. _Basic:_ Communication. _Not essential:_ Artistic, interpersonal, managerial. **Education and training:** Moderate-term on-the-job training. **Annual earnings:** $27,717. **Annual openings:** 127,000. **Job growth through 2012:** 4.9%.

❑ **Machinists**
Set up and operate a variety of machine tools to produce precision parts and instruments. Fabricate, modify, or repair mechanical instruments or parts of machine tools. **Skill levels:** _High:_ Mathematics, mechanical. _Moderate:_ Artistic, science. _Basic:_ Communication. _Not essential:_ Interpersonal, managerial. **Education and training:** Long-term on-the-job training. **Annual earnings:** $33,960. **Annual openings:** 30,000. **Job growth through 2012:** 8.2%.

❑ **Tool and Die Makers**
Analyze specifications, lay out metal stock, set up and operate machine tools, and fit and assemble parts to make and repair dies, cutting tools, jigs, fixtures, gauges, and machinists' hand tools. **Skill levels:** _High:_ Mathematics, mechanical. _Moderate:_ Science. _Basic:_ Artistic, communication. _Not essential:_ Interpersonal, managerial. **Education and training:** Long-term on-the-job training. **Annual earnings:** $42,740. **Annual openings:** 3,000. **Job growth through 2012:** 0.4%.

Production Precision Work

❑ **Assemblers and Fabricators**
Produce a wide range of finished goods, such as aircraft, automobile engines, computers, and electrical and electronic components, from manufactured parts or subassemblies. **Skill levels:** _High:_ Mechanical. _Basic:_ Artistic, communication, mathematics, science. _Not essential:_ Interpersonal, managerial. **Education and training:** Moderate-term on-the-job training. **Annual earnings:** $24,840. **Annual openings:** 193,000. **Job growth through 2012:** –4.3%.

❑ **Bookbinders and Bindery Workers**
Set up or operate binding machines that produce books and other printed materials, or perform highly skilled hand finishing operations, such as grooving and lettering, to bind books. **Skill levels:** _High:_ Mechanical. _Basic:_ Artistic, communication, mathematics, science. _Not essential:_ Interpersonal,

managerial. **Education and training:** Moderate-term on-the-job training. **Annual earnings:** $23,878. **Annual openings:** 6,000. **Job growth through 2012:** –4.7%.

❑ **Dental Laboratory Technicians**
Construct and repair full or partial dentures or dental appliances. **Skill levels:** *High:* Mechanical. *Moderate:* Artistic, science. *Basic:* Communication, mathematics. *Not essential:* Interpersonal, managerial. **Education and training:** Long-term on-the-job training. **Annual earnings:** $31,060. **Annual openings:** 3,000. **Job growth through 2012:** 3.6%.

❑ **Jewelers and Precious Stones and Metal Workers**
Design, fabricate, adjust, repair, or appraise jewelry, gold, silver, other precious metals, or gems. **Skill levels:** *High:* Artistic, mechanical. *Moderate:* Science. *Basic:* Communication, interpersonal, mathematics. *Not essential:* Managerial. **Education and training:** Postsecondary vocational award. **Annual earnings:** $27,400. **Annual openings:** 3,000. **Job growth through 2012:** 4.5%.

❑ **Ophthalmic Laboratory Technicians**
Make prescription eyeglass or contact lenses. Cut, grind, edge, and finish lenses according to specifications provided by dispensing opticians, optometrists, or ophthalmologists. May insert lenses into frames to produce finished glasses. **Skill levels:** *High:* Mechanical. *Moderate:* Interpersonal, science. *Basic:* Artistic, communication, mathematics. *Not essential:* Managerial. **Education and training:** Moderate-term on-the-job training. **Annual earnings:** $23,710. **Annual openings:** 2,000. **Job growth through 2012:** 9.2%.

❑ **Semiconductor Processors**
Perform tasks necessary in the manufacture of electronic semiconductors (also known as computer chips, microchips, or integrated circuits). **Skill levels:** *High:* Mathematics, science. *Moderate:* Mechanical. *Basic:* Communication. *Not essential:* Artistic, interpersonal, managerial. **Education and training:** Associate degree. **Annual earnings:** $28,810. **Annual openings:** 4,000. **Job growth through 2012:** –10.6%.

Production Quality Control

❑ **Agricultural Workers**
Plant and harvest crops, install irrigation, deliver animals, and make sure that food is safe. **Skill levels:** *High:* Mechanical. *Basic:* Communication, interpersonal, managerial, mathematics, science. *Not essential:* Artistic.

Education and training: Moderate-term on-the-job training. **Annual earnings:** $18,676. **Annual openings:** 40,000. **Job growth through 2012:** 6.2%.

❏ **Inspectors, Testers, Sorters, Samplers, and Weighers**
Inspect, test, sort, sample, or weigh nonagricultural raw materials or processed, machined, fabricated, or assembled parts or products for defects, wear, and deviations from specifications. **Skill levels:** *High:* Mechanical. *Moderate:* Communication, mathematics, science. *Basic:* Artistic, interpersonal. *Not essential:* Managerial. **Education and training:** Moderate-term on-the-job training. **Annual earnings:** $28,410. **Annual openings:** 87,000. **Job growth through 2012:** 4.7%.

Graphic Arts Production
❏ **Bookbinders and Bindery Workers**
Set up or operate binding machines that produce books and other printed materials, or perform highly skilled hand finishing operations, such as grooving and lettering, to bind books. **Skill levels:** *High:* Mechanical. *Basic:* Artistic, communication, mathematics, science. *Not essential:* Interpersonal, managerial. **Education and training:** Moderate-term on-the-job training. **Annual earnings:** $23,878. **Annual openings:** 6,000. **Job growth through 2012:** –4.7%.

❏ **Desktop Publishers**
Format typescript and graphic elements using computer software to produce publication-ready material. **Skill levels:** *High:* Artistic. *Moderate:* Mechanical. *Basic:* Communication, interpersonal, mathematics, science. *Not essential:* Managerial. **Education and training:** Postsecondary vocational award. **Annual earnings:** $32,340. **Annual openings:** 4,000. **Job growth through 2012:** 29.2%.

❏ **Photographic Process Workers and Processing Machine Operators**
Perform precision work involved in photographic processing, such as editing photographic negatives and prints; using photo-mechanical, chemical, or computerized methods; or operating photographic processing machines. **Skill levels:** *High:* Mechanical. *Basic:* Artistic, communication, mathematics, science. *Not essential:* Interpersonal, managerial. **Education and training:** Short-term on-the-job training. **Annual earnings:** $19,619. **Annual openings:** 13,000. **Job growth through 2012:** 7.9%.

❏ **Prepress Technicians and Workers**

Set up and prepare material for printing presses. Include prepress functions, such as compositing, typesetting, layout, paste-up, camera operating, scanning, film stripping, and photoengraving. **Skill levels:** *Moderate:* Artistic, communication, mathematics, mechanical. *Basic:* Interpersonal, science. *Not essential:* Managerial. **Education and training:** Long-term on-the-job training. **Annual earnings:** $31,918. **Annual openings:** 13,000. **Job growth through 2012:** –3.4%.

❏ **Printing Machine Operators**

Set up or operate various types of printing machines, such as offset, letterset, intaglio, or gravure presses or screen printers to produce print on paper or other materials. **Skill levels:** *High:* Mechanical. *Basic:* Communication, mathematics, science. *Not essential:* Artistic, interpersonal, managerial. **Education and training:** Moderate-term on-the-job training. **Annual earnings:** $29,900. **Annual openings:** 30,000. **Job growth through 2012:** 4.6%.

Hands-On Work, Assorted Materials

❏ **Assemblers and Fabricators**

Produce a wide range of finished goods, such as aircraft, automobile engines, computers, and electrical and electronic components, from manufactured parts or subassemblies. **Skill levels:** *High:* Mechanical. *Basic:* Artistic, communication, mathematics, science. *Not essential:* Interpersonal, managerial. **Education and training:** Moderate-term on-the-job training. **Annual earnings:** $24,840. **Annual openings:** 193,000. **Job growth through 2012:** –4.3%.

❏ **Painting and Coating Workers, Except Construction and Maintenance**

Control the machinery that applies paints and coatings to a wide range of manufactured products. May dip an item in a large vat of paint or other coating or spray products with a solution of paint or some other coating. **Skill levels:** *High:* Mechanical. *Basic:* Artistic, communication, mathematics. *Not essential:* Interpersonal, managerial, science. **Education and training:** Moderate-term on-the-job training. **Annual earnings:** $28,016. **Annual openings:** 32,000. **Job growth through 2012:** 13.1%.

❏ **Textile, Apparel, and Furnishings Occupations**

Produce textile and leather materials and fashion them into a wide range of garment and nongarment products. May operate large industrial machinery, smaller power equipment, or do substantial handwork. **Skill levels:**

High: Mechanical. *Moderate:* Artistic. *Basic:* Communication, mathematics. *Not essential:* Interpersonal, managerial, science. **Education and training:** Moderate-term on-the-job training. **Annual earnings:** $19,619. **Annual openings:** 161,000. **Job growth through 2012:** –15.1%.

Woodworking Technology

❑ **Woodworkers**

Play a role in processing wood into finished products. May produce structural elements of buildings; mill hardwood and softwood lumber; assemble finished wood products; or operate machines that cut, shape, assemble, and finish raw wood. **Skill levels:** *High:* Mechanical. *Moderate:* Artistic, mathematics. *Basic:* Communication, science. *Not essential:* Interpersonal, managerial. **Education and training:** Long-term on-the-job training. **Annual earnings:** $24,062. **Annual openings:** 42,000. **Job growth through 2012:** 5.4%.

Apparel, Shoes, Leather, and Fabric Care

❑ **Textile, Apparel, and Furnishings Occupations**

Produce textile and leather materials and fashion them into a wide range of garment and nongarment products. May operate large industrial machinery, smaller power equipment, or do substantial handwork. **Skill levels:** *High:* Mechanical. *Moderate:* Artistic. *Basic:* Communication, mathematics. *Not essential:* Interpersonal, managerial, science. **Education and training:** Moderate-term on-the-job training. **Annual earnings:** $19,619. **Annual openings:** 161,000. **Job growth through 2012:** –15.1%.

Electrical and Electronic Repair

❑ **Aircraft and Avionics Equipment Mechanics and Service Technicians**

Diagnose, adjust, repair, or overhaul aircraft engines and assemblies, such as hydraulic and pneumatic systems, or install, inspect, test, adjust, or repair avionics (aircraft electronics equipment). **Skill levels:** *High:* Mechanical. *Moderate:* Mathematics, science. *Basic:* Communication, interpersonal. *Not essential:* Artistic, managerial. **Education and training:** Postsecondary vocational award. **Annual earnings:** $45,144. **Annual openings:** 15,000. **Job growth through 2012:** 9.9%.

❑ **Electrical and Electronic Installers and Repairers**

Install, maintain, and repair complex electronic equipment. Use software programs and testing equipment to diagnose malfunctions. Use hand tools to replace faulty parts and adjust equipment. **Skill levels:** *High:*

Mechanical. *Moderate:* Mathematics. *Basic:* Communication, interpersonal, science. *Not essential:* Artistic, managerial. **Education and training:** Postsecondary vocational award. **Annual earnings:** $40,186. **Annual openings:** 18,000. **Job growth through 2012:** 8.2%.

❑ **Electronic Home Entertainment Equipment Repairers**
Repair, adjust, or install audio or television receivers, stereo systems, camcorders, video systems, or other electronic home entertainment equipment. **Skill levels:** *High:* Mechanical. *Moderate:* Artistic, mathematics. *Basic:* Communication, interpersonal, science. *Not essential:* Managerial. **Education and training:** Postsecondary vocational award. **Annual earnings:** $27,960. **Annual openings:** 5,000. **Job growth through 2012:** 8.6%.

❑ **Radio and Telecommunications Equipment Installers and Repairers**
Set up and maintain equipment such as switches and cables in central telecommunications offices, private branch exchange (PBX) switchboards, telephone wiring and equipment on customers' premises, and radio transmitting and receiving equipment. **Skill levels:** *High:* Mechanical. *Moderate:* Mathematics, science. *Basic:* Communication, interpersonal. *Not essential:* Artistic, managerial. **Education and training:** Long-term on-the-job training. **Annual earnings:** $49,434. **Annual openings:** 24,000. **Job growth through 2012:** –1.5%.

Machinery Repair

❑ **Electrical and Electronic Installers and Repairers**
Install, maintain, and repair complex electronic equipment. Use software programs and testing equipment to diagnose malfunctions. Use hand tools to replace faulty parts and adjust equipment. **Skill levels:** *High:* Mechanical. *Moderate:* Mathematics. *Basic:* Communication, interpersonal, science. *Not essential:* Artistic, managerial. **Education and training:** Postsecondary vocational award. **Annual earnings:** $40,186. **Annual openings:** 18,000. **Job growth through 2012:** 8.2%.

❑ **Home Appliance Repairers**
Repair, adjust, or install all types of electric or gas household appliances, such as refrigerators, washers, dryers, and ovens. **Skill levels:** *High:* Mechanical. *Basic:* Communication, interpersonal, mathematics, science. *Not essential:* Artistic, managerial. **Education and training:** Long-term on-the-job training. **Annual earnings:** $32,180. **Annual openings:** 5,000. **Job growth through 2012:** 5.5%.

❑ **Industrial Machinery Installation, Repair, and Maintenance Workers, except Millwright**

Repair, install, adjust, or maintain industrial production and processing machinery or refinery and pipeline distribution systems. **Skill levels:** *High:* Mechanical. *Basic:* Communication, mathematics, science. *Not essential:* Artistic, interpersonal, managerial. **Education and training:** Moderate-term on-the-job training. **Annual earnings:** $31,894. **Annual openings:** 22,262. **Job growth through 2012:** 14.3%.

❑ **Millwrights**

Install, dismantle, or move machinery and heavy equipment according to layout plans, blueprints, or other drawings. **Skill levels:** *High:* Mechanical. *Moderate:* Mathematics. *Basic:* Communication, interpersonal, science. *Not essential:* Artistic, managerial. **Education and training:** Long-term on-the-job training. **Annual earnings:** $43,720. **Annual openings:** 7,000. **Job growth through 2012:** 5.3%.

Vehicle and Facility Mechanical Work

❑ **Aircraft and Avionics Equipment Mechanics and Service Technicians**

Diagnose, adjust, repair, or overhaul aircraft engines and assemblies, such as hydraulic and pneumatic systems, or install, inspect, test, adjust, or repair avionics (aircraft electronics equipment). **Skill levels:** *High:* Mechanical. *Moderate:* Mathematics, science. *Basic:* Communication, interpersonal. *Not essential:* Artistic, managerial. **Education and training:** Postsecondary vocational award. **Annual earnings:** $45,144. **Annual openings:** 15,000. **Job growth through 2012:** 9.9%.

❑ **Assemblers and Fabricators**

Produce a wide range of finished goods, such as aircraft, automobile engines, computers, and electrical and electronic components, from manufactured parts or subassemblies. **Skill levels:** *High:* Mechanical. *Basic:* Artistic, communication, mathematics, science. *Not essential:* Interpersonal, managerial. **Education and training:** Moderate-term on-the-job training. **Annual earnings:** $24,840. **Annual openings:** 193,000. **Job growth through 2012:** –4.3%.

❑ **Automotive Body and Related Repairers**

Repair and refinish automotive vehicle bodies and straighten vehicle frames, or replace or repair broken windshields and window glass in motor vehicles. **Skill levels:** *High:* Mechanical. *Basic:* Artistic, communication, interpersonal, mathematics, science. *Not essential:* Managerial. **Education**

and training: Long-term on-the-job training. **Annual earnings:** $34,018. **Annual openings:** 26,000. **Job growth through 2012:** 13.0%.

❑ **Automotive Service Technicians and Mechanics**
Diagnose, adjust, repair, or overhaul automotive vehicles. **Skill levels:** *High:* Mechanical. *Moderate:* Science. *Basic:* Communication, interpersonal, mathematics. *Not essential:* Artistic, managerial. **Education and training:** Postsecondary vocational award. **Annual earnings:** $32,450. **Annual openings:** 100,000. **Job growth through 2012:** 12.4%.

❑ **Diesel Service Technicians and Mechanics**
Diagnose, adjust, repair, or overhaul all types of diesel engines, including those used in trucks, buses, and automobiles. **Skill levels:** *High:* Mechanical. *Moderate:* Science. *Basic:* Communication, interpersonal, mathematics. *Not essential:* Artistic, managerial. **Education and training:** Postsecondary vocational award. **Annual earnings:** $35,780. **Annual openings:** 28,000. **Job growth through 2012:** 14.2%.

❑ **Heavy Vehicle and Mobile Equipment Service Technicians and Mechanics**
Perform routine maintenance checks on diesel engines and on fuel, brake, and transmission systems to ensure peak performance, safety, and longevity of the equipment. Using hand-held tools, repair, replace, clean, and lubricate parts as necessary. **Skill levels:** *High:* Mechanical. *Moderate:* Science. *Basic:* Communication, interpersonal, mathematics. *Not essential:* Artistic, managerial. **Education and training:** Postsecondary vocational award. **Annual earnings:** $36,305. **Annual openings:** 1,547. **Job growth through 2012:** 8.8%.

❑ **Small Engine Mechanics**
Repair and service power equipment ranging from racing motorcycles to chain saws. **Skill levels:** *High:* Mechanical. *Moderate:* Science. *Basic:* Communication, interpersonal, mathematics. *Not essential:* Artistic, managerial. **Education and training:** Moderate-term on-the-job training. **Annual earnings:** $26,107. **Annual openings:** 4,000. **Job growth through 2012:** 18.8%.

Medical and Technical Equipment Repair

❑ **Precision Instrument and Equipment Repairers**
Repair and maintain watches, cameras, musical instruments, medical equipment, or other precision instruments. May machine or fabricate a new part. For preventive maintenance may perform regular lubrication,

cleaning, and adjustment. **Skill levels:** *High:* Mechanical. *Moderate:* Mathematics. *Basic:* Artistic, communication, science. *Not essential:* Interpersonal, managerial. **Education and training:** Associate degree. **Annual earnings:** $34,427. **Annual openings:** 7,000. **Job growth through 2012:** 9.3%.

Utility Operation and Energy Distribution

❑ **Material Moving Occupations**

Use machinery to move construction materials, earth, petroleum products, and other heavy materials, generally over short distances; manually handle freight, stock, or other materials; clean equipment; or feed materials into processing machinery. **Skill levels:** *High:* Mechanical. *Basic:* Communication. *Not essential:* Artistic, interpersonal, managerial, mathematics, science. **Education and training:** Moderate-term on-the-job training. **Annual earnings:** $26,896. **Annual openings:** 930,000. **Job growth through 2012:** –1.5%.

❑ **Power Plant Operators, Distributors, and Dispatchers**

Control machinery that generates electricity or the flow of electricity from the power plant, over a network of transmission lines, to industrial plants and substations, and, finally, over distribution lines to residential users. **Skill levels:** *High:* Mathematics, science. *Moderate:* Interpersonal. *Basic:* Communication, managerial, mechanical. *Not essential:* Artistic. **Education and training:** Long-term on-the-job training. **Annual earnings:** $54,376. **Annual openings:** 4,000. **Job growth through 2012:** –0.7%.

❑ **Stationary Engineers and Boiler Operators**

Operate or maintain stationary engines, boilers, or other mechanical equipment to provide utilities for buildings or industrial processes. **Skill levels:** *High:* Mechanical. *Basic:* Communication, interpersonal, managerial, mathematics, science. *Not essential:* Artistic. **Education and training:** Long-term on-the-job training. **Annual earnings:** $44,150. **Annual openings:** 4,000. **Job growth through 2012:** 0.3%.

❑ **Water and Liquid Waste Treatment Plant and System Operators**

Operate or control an entire process or system of machines, often through the use of control boards, to transfer or treat water or liquid waste. **Skill levels:** *High:* Mechanical. *Moderate:* Mathematics, science. *Basic:* Communication, interpersonal, managerial. *Not essential:* Artistic. **Education and training:** Long-term on-the-job training. **Annual earnings:** $34,960. **Annual openings:** 9,000. **Job growth through 2012:** 16.0%.

❑ **Water Transportation Occupations**
Operate and maintain deep-sea merchant ships, tugboats, towboats, ferries, dredges, excursion vessels, and other waterborne craft on the oceans, the Great Lakes, rivers, canals, and other waterways, as well as in harbors. **Skill levels:** *High:* Managerial, mechanical. *Moderate:* Communication, mathematics, science. *Basic:* Interpersonal. *Not essential:* Artistic. **Education and training:** Moderate-term on-the-job training. **Annual earnings:** $40,819. **Annual openings:** 8,000. **Job growth through 2012:** 3.4%.

Loading, Moving, Hoisting, and Conveying

❑ **Hazardous Materials Removal Workers**
Identify, remove, pack, transport, or dispose of hazardous materials, including asbestos, lead-based paint, waste oil, fuel, transmission fluid, radioactive materials, and contaminated soil. **Skill levels:** *High:* Mechanical, science. *Basic:* Communication, interpersonal, mathematics. *Not essential:* Artistic, managerial. **Education and training:** Moderate-term on-the-job training. **Annual earnings:** $33,320. **Annual openings:** 8,000. **Job growth through 2012:** 43.1%.

❑ **Material Moving Occupations**
Use machinery to move construction materials, earth, petroleum products, and other heavy materials, generally over short distances; manually handle freight, stock, or other materials; clean equipment; or feed materials into processing machinery. **Skill levels:** *High:* Mechanical. *Basic:* Communication. *Not essential:* Artistic, interpersonal, managerial, mathematics, science. **Education and training:** Moderate-term on-the-job training. **Annual earnings:** $26,896. **Annual openings:** 930,000. **Job growth through 2012:** –1.5%.

14. Retail and Wholesale Sales and Service

Managerial Work in Retail/Wholesale Sales and Service

❑ **Advertising, Marketing, Promotions, Public Relations, and Sales Managers**
Coordinate market research, marketing strategy, sales, advertising, promotion, pricing, product development, and public relations activities. Oversee advertising and promotion staffs. **Skill levels:** *High:* Artistic, communication, interpersonal, managerial, mathematics. *Moderate:* Mechanical. *Not essential:* Science. **Education and training:** Work experience plus degree. **Annual earnings:** $82,252. **Annual openings:** 107,000. **Job growth through 2012:** 26.5%.

❏ **Funeral Directors**

Perform various tasks to arrange and direct funeral services, such as coordinating transportation of body to mortuary for embalming, interviewing family to arrange details, selecting pallbearers, and procuring official for religious rites. **Skill levels:** *High:* Communication, interpersonal. *Moderate:* Managerial, mathematics. *Basic:* Artistic, mechanical, science. *Not essential:* **Education and training:** Associate degree. **Annual earnings:** $45,960. **Annual openings:** 3,000. **Job growth through 2012:** 6.6%.

❏ **Property, Real Estate, and Community Association Managers**

Plan, direct, or coordinate selling, buying, leasing, or governance activities of commercial, industrial, or residential real estate properties. **Skill levels:** *High:* Communication, interpersonal, managerial. *Basic:* Artistic, mathematics, mechanical. *Not essential:* Science. **Education and training:** Bachelor's degree. **Annual earnings:** $39,980. **Annual openings:** 35,000. **Job growth through 2012:** 12.8%.

❏ **Purchasing Managers, Buyers, and Purchasing Agents**

Seek to obtain the highest quality merchandise at the lowest possible purchase cost for employers. Buy goods and services for use by a company or organization, or buy items for resale. **Skill levels:** *High:* Communication, interpersonal, managerial. *Moderate:* Mathematics. *Basic:* Science. *Not essential:* Artistic, mechanical. **Education and training:** Work experience in a related occupation. **Annual earnings:** $51,010. **Annual openings:** 64,000. **Job growth through 2012:** 7.8%.

❏ **Sales Worker Supervisors**

Oversee the work of sales and related workers, such as retail salespersons, cashiers, customer service representatives, stock clerks and order fillers, sales engineers, and wholesale and manufacturing sales representatives. **Skill levels:** *High:* Communication, interpersonal, managerial. *Moderate:* Mathematics. *Basic:* Artistic, mechanical, science. **Education and training:** Work experience in a related occupation. **Annual earnings:** $39,346. **Annual openings:** 323,000. **Job growth through 2012:** 8.5%.

Technical Sales

❏ **Sales Engineers**

Using engineering skills, help customers determine products or services that best suit their needs. May work with both the customer and the employer to plan new or improved products and services. **Skill levels:** *High:* Communication, interpersonal. *Moderate:* Mathematics, science. *Basic:* Artistic, mechanical. *Not essential:* Managerial. **Education and**

training: Bachelor's degree. **Annual earnings:** $70,620. **Annual openings:** 7,000. **Job growth through 2012:** 19.9%.

❏ **Sales Representatives, Wholesale and Manufacturing**
Represent one or several manufacturers or wholesale distributors by selling one product or a complementary line of products. Advise clients on methods to reduce costs, use manufacturer's products, and increase sales. **Skill levels:** *High:* Communication, interpersonal. *Moderate:* Mathematics. *Basic:* Artistic, science. *Not essential:* Managerial, mechanical. **Education and training:** Moderate-term on-the-job training. **Annual earnings:** $48,225. **Annual openings:** 204,000. **Job growth through 2012:** 19.1%.

General Sales

❏ **Real Estate Brokers and Sales Agents**
Rent, buy, or sell property for clients. Perform duties such as study property listings, interview prospective clients, accompany clients to property site, discuss conditions of sale, and draw up real estate contracts. **Skill levels:** *High:* Communication, interpersonal. *Moderate:* Managerial, mathematics. *Basic:* Artistic. *Not essential:* Mechanical, science. **Education and training:** Postsecondary vocational award. **Annual earnings:** $41,277. **Annual openings:** 45,000. **Job growth through 2012:** 4.9%.

❏ **Retail Salespersons**
Sell merchandise, such as furniture, motor vehicles, appliances, or apparel in a retail establishment. **Skill levels:** *High:* Interpersonal. *Moderate:* Communication. *Basic:* Artistic, mathematics. *Not essential:* Managerial, mechanical, science. **Education and training:** Short-term on-the-job training. **Annual earnings:** $18,680. **Annual openings:** 1,014,000. **Job growth through 2012:** 14.6%.

Personal Soliciting

❏ **Demonstrators, Product Promoters, and Models**
Demonstrate merchandise and answer questions for the purpose of creating public interest in buying the product, or model garments and other apparel to display clothing before prospective buyers. **Skill levels:** *High:* Artistic, communication, interpersonal. *Basic:* Mathematics, mechanical. *Not essential:* Managerial, science. **Education and training:** Moderate-term on-the-job training. **Annual earnings:** $33,670. **Annual openings:** 39,000. **Job growth through 2012:** 16.9%.

Purchasing

❏ **Purchasing Managers, Buyers, and Purchasing Agents**

Seek to obtain the highest quality merchandise at the lowest possible purchase cost for employers. Buy goods and services for use by a company or organization, or buy items for resale. **Skill levels:** *High:* Communication, interpersonal, managerial. *Moderate:* Mathematics. *Basic:* Science. *Not essential:* Artistic, mechanical. **Education and training:** Work experience in a related occupation. **Annual earnings:** $51,010. **Annual openings:** 64,000. **Job growth through 2012:** 7.8%.

Customer Service

❏ **Cashiers**

Receive and disburse money in establishments other than financial institutions. Usually involves use of electronic scanners, cash registers, or related equipment. Often involved in processing credit or debit card transactions and validating checks. **Skill levels:** *Moderate:* Interpersonal, mathematics. *Basic:* Communication. *Not essential:* Artistic, managerial, mechanical, science. **Education and training:** Short-term on-the-job training. **Annual earnings:** $16,281. **Annual openings:** 1,233,000. **Job growth through 2012:** 13.3%.

❏ **Counter and Rental Clerks**

Receive orders for repairs, rentals, and services. May describe available options, compute cost, and accept payment. **Skill levels:** *Moderate:* Interpersonal, mathematics. *Basic:* Communication. *Not essential:* Artistic, managerial, mechanical, science. **Education and training:** Short-term on-the-job training. **Annual earnings:** $18,280. **Annual openings:** 144,000. **Job growth through 2012:** 26.3%.

❏ **Customer Service Representatives**

Interact with customers to provide information in response to inquiries about products or services and to handle and resolve complaints. Serve as a direct point of contact for customers. **Skill levels:** *High:* Communication, interpersonal. *Moderate:* Mathematics. *Basic:* Science. *Not essential:* Artistic, managerial, mechanical. **Education and training:** Moderate-term on-the-job training. **Annual earnings:** $27,020. **Annual openings:** 419,000. **Job growth through 2012:** 24.3%.

❑ **Information and Record Clerks**
Gather data and provide information to the public. Greet customers, guests, or other visitors. May answer telephones. **Skill levels:** *Moderate:* Communication, mathematics. *Basic:* Interpersonal. *Not essential:* Artistic, managerial, mechanical, science. **Education and training:** Moderate-term on-the-job training. **Annual earnings:** $26,402. **Annual openings:** 585,000. **Job growth through 2012:** 17.8%.

❑ **Order Clerks**
Receive and process incoming orders for materials, merchandise, classified ads, or services such as repairs, installations, or rental of facilities. **Skill levels:** *Moderate:* Mathematics. *Basic:* Communication, interpersonal. *Not essential:* Artistic, managerial, mechanical, science. **Education and training:** Short-term on-the-job training. **Annual earnings:** $25,110. Annual openings: 61,000. **Job growth through 2012:** –5.7.

❑ **Receptionists and Information Clerks**
Answer inquiries and obtain information for general public, customers, visitors, and other interested parties. Provide information regarding activities conducted at establishment, such as location of departments and offices and employees within organization. **Skill levels:** *High:* Communication, interpersonal. *Moderate:* Mathematics, mechanical. *Not essential:* Artistic, managerial, science. **Education and training:** Short-term on-the-job training. **Annual earnings:** $21,830. **Annual openings:** 296,000. **Job growth through 2012:** 29.5%.

15. Scientific Research, Engineering, and Mathematics

Managerial Work in Scientific Research, Engineering, and Mathematics

❑ **Engineering and Natural Sciences Managers**
Plan, coordinate, and direct research, design, and production activities. May supervise engineers, scientists, and technicians, along with support personnel. Use advanced technical knowledge of engineering and science to oversee a variety of activities. **Skill levels:** *High:* Communication, interpersonal, managerial, mathematics, mechanical, science. *Not essential:* Artistic. **Education and training:** Work experience plus degree. **Annual earnings:** $33,670. **Annual openings:** 21,000. **Job growth through 2012:** 9.6%.

Physical Sciences

❑ **Atmospheric Scientists**

Investigate atmospheric phenomena and interpret meteorological data gathered by surface and air stations, satellites, and radar to prepare reports and forecasts for public and other uses. **Skill levels:** *High:* Mathematics, mechanical, science. *Moderate:* Communication, managerial. *Basic:* Interpersonal. *Not essential:* Artistic. **Education and training:** Bachelor's degree. **Annual earnings:** $70,100. **Annual openings:** 1,000. **Job growth through 2012:** 16.2%.

❑ **Chemists and Materials Scientists**

Conduct qualitative and quantitative chemical analyses or chemical experiments in laboratories for quality or process control or to develop new products or knowledge. May research and study the structures and chemical properties of various materials. **Skill levels:** *High:* Mathematics, mechanical, science. *Moderate:* Communication, managerial. *Basic:* Artistic, interpersonal. **Education and training:** Bachelor's degree. **Annual earnings:** $57,316. **Annual openings:** 8,000. **Job growth through 2012:** 12.4%.

❑ **Environmental Scientists and Geoscientists**

Use knowledge of the physical makeup and history of the Earth to protect the environment; locate water, mineral, and energy resources; predict future geologic hazards; and offer advice on construction and land-use projects. **Skill levels:** *High:* Mathematics, mechanical, science. *Moderate:* Communication, managerial. *Basic:* Artistic, interpersonal. **Education and training:** Master's degree. **Annual earnings:** $56,799. **Annual openings:** 9,000. **Job growth through 2012:** 20.1%.

❑ **Physicists and Astronomers**

Conduct research into the phases of physical phenomena, develop theories and laws on the basis of observation and experiments, and devise methods to apply laws and theories to industry and other fields. May specialize in celestial phenomena. **Skill levels:** *High:* Mathematics, mechanical, science. *Moderate:* Communication. *Basic:* Artistic, interpersonal, managerial. **Education and training:** Doctoral degree. **Annual earnings:** $88,155. **Annual openings:** 1,000. **Job growth through 2012:** 6.8%.

❑ **Social Scientists, Other**

Study various aspects of society to understand how individuals and groups make decisions, exercise power, and respond to change. Suggest solutions to social, business, personal, governmental, and environmental problems.

Skill levels: *Moderate:* Communication, interpersonal, mathematics. *Basic:* Managerial, mechanical, science. *Not essential:* Artistic. **Education and training:** Master's degree. **Annual earnings:** $62,442. **Annual openings:** 2,000. **Job growth through 2012:** 10.1%.

Life Sciences

❑ **Biological Scientists**

Study living organisms and their relationship to their environment; research problems dealing with life processes; usually specialize in some area of biology, such as zoology (the study of animals) or microbiology (the study of microscopic organisms). **Skill levels:** *High:* Mathematics, mechanical, science. *Moderate:* Communication, managerial. *Basic:* Interpersonal. *Not essential:* Artistic. **Education and training:** Doctoral degree. **Annual earnings:** $58,428. **Annual openings:** 4,000. **Job growth through 2012:** 17.2%.

❑ **Environmental Scientists and Geoscientists**

Use knowledge of the physical makeup and history of the Earth to protect the environment; locate water, mineral, and energy resources; predict future geologic hazards; and offer advice on construction and land-use projects. **Skill levels:** *High:* Mathematics, mechanical, science. *Moderate:* Communication, managerial. *Basic:* Artistic, interpersonal. **Education and training:** Master's degree. **Annual earnings:** $56,799. **Annual openings:** 9,000. **Job growth through 2012:** 20.1%.

❑ **Medical Scientists**

Research human diseases in order to improve human health. Study biological systems to understand the causes of disease and other health problems and to develop treatments. **Skill levels:** *High:* Mathematics, mechanical, science. *Moderate:* Communication, managerial. *Basic:* Interpersonal. *Not essential:* Artistic. **Education and training:** Doctoral degree. **Annual earnings:** $60,899. **Annual openings:** 6,000. **Job growth through 2012:** 27.3%.

Social Sciences

❑ **Economists**

Conduct research, prepare reports, or formulate plans to aid in solution of economic problems arising from production and distribution of goods and services. May collect and process economic and statistical data using econometric and sampling techniques. **Skill levels:** *High:* Mathematics.

Moderate: Communication, managerial. *Basic:* Interpersonal. *Not essential:* Artistic, mechanical, science. **Education and training:** Master's degree. **Annual earnings:** $72,780. **Annual openings:** 2,000. **Job growth through 2012:** 13.4%.

❑ **Psychologists**

Study the human mind and human behavior. In research, investigate the physical, cognitive, emotional, or social aspects of human behavior. In health service provider fields, provide mental health care in hospitals, clinics, schools, or private settings. **Skill levels:** *High:* Communication, interpersonal. *Moderate:* Mathematics, science. *Basic:* Managerial. *Not essential:* Artistic, mechanical. **Education and training:** Doctoral degree. **Annual earnings:** $55,187. **Annual openings:** 17,000. **Job growth through 2012:** 24.3%.

❑ **Social Scientists, Other**

Study various aspects of society to understand how individuals and groups make decisions, exercise power, and respond to change. Suggest solutions to social, business, personal, governmental, and environmental problems. **Skill levels:** *Moderate:* Communication, interpersonal, mathematics. *Basic:* Managerial, mechanical, science. *Not essential:* Artistic. **Education and training:** Master's degree. **Annual earnings:** $62,442. **Annual openings:** 2,000. **Job growth through 2012:** 10.1%.

Physical Science Laboratory Technology

❑ **Photographers**

Photograph persons, subjects, merchandise, or other commercial products. May develop negatives and produce finished prints. **Skill levels:** *High:* Artistic, mechanical. *Basic:* Communication, interpersonal, managerial, mathematics, science. **Education and training:** Long-term on-the-job training. **Annual earnings:** $26,080. **Annual openings:** 18,000. **Job growth through 2012:** 13.6%.

Mathematics and Data Analysis

❑ **Actuaries**

Analyze statistical data, such as mortality, accident, sickness, disability, and retirement rates and construct probability tables to forecast risk and liability for payment of future benefits. **Skill levels:** *High:* Mathematics. *Moderate:* Science. *Basic:* Communication, interpersonal, managerial. *Not* *essential:* Artistic, mechanical. **Education and training:** Work experience plus degree. **Annual earnings:** $76,340. **Annual openings:** 2,000. **Job growth through 2012:** 14.9%.

❏ **Mathematicians**

Conduct research in fundamental mathematics or in application of mathematical techniques to science, management, and other fields. Solve or direct solutions to problems in various fields by mathematical methods. **Skill levels:** *High:* Mathematics. *Moderate:* Science. *Basic:* Communication, interpersonal, managerial. *Not essential:* Artistic, mechanical. **Education and training:** Master's degree. **Annual earnings:** $81,240. **Annual openings:** fewer than 500. **Job growth through 2012:** −1.0%.

❏ **Statisticians**

Engage in the development of mathematical theory or apply statistical theory and methods to collect, organize, interpret, and summarize numerical data to provide usable information. **Skill levels:** *High:* Mathematics. *Moderate:* Science. *Basic:* Communication, interpersonal, managerial. *Not essential:* Artistic, mechanical. **Education and training:** Master's degree. **Annual earnings:** $58,620. **Annual openings:** 2,000. **Job growth through 2012:** 4.8%.

Research and Design Engineering

❏ **Aerospace Engineers**

Perform a variety of engineering work in designing, constructing, and testing aircraft, missiles, and spacecraft. May conduct basic and applied research to evaluate adaptability of materials and equipment to aircraft design and manufacture. **Skill levels:** *High:* Mathematics, mechanical, science. *Moderate:* Communication, managerial. *Basic:* Artistic, interpersonal. **Education and training:** Bachelor's degree. **Annual earnings:** $79,100. **Annual openings:** 5,000. **Job growth through 2012:** −5.2%.

❏ **Biomedical Engineers**

Combine biology and medicine with engineering to develop devices and procedures that solve medical and health-related problems. May do research along with life scientists, chemists, and medical scientists. **Skill levels:** *High:* Mathematics, mechanical, science. *Moderate:* Communication, managerial. *Basic:* Artistic, interpersonal. **Education and training:** Bachelor's degree. **Annual earnings:** $67,690. **Annual openings:** fewer than 500. **Job growth through 2012:** 26.1%.

❑ **Chemical Engineers**

Design chemical plant equipment and devise processes for manufacturing chemicals and products, such as gasoline, synthetic rubber, plastics, detergents, cement, paper, and pulp, by applying principles and technology of chemistry, physics, and engineering. **Skill levels:** *High:* Mathematics, mechanical, science. *Moderate:* Communication, managerial. *Basic:* Artistic, interpersonal. **Education and training:** Bachelor's degree. **Annual earnings:** $76,770. **Annual openings:** 2,000. **Job growth through 2012:** 0.4%.

❑ **Civil Engineers**

Perform engineering duties in planning, designing, and overseeing construction and maintenance of structures and facilities such as roads, railroads, airports, bridges, harbors, channels, dams, pipelines, and power plants. **Skill levels:** *High:* Mathematics, mechanical, science. *Moderate:* Artistic, communication, managerial. *Basic:* Interpersonal. **Education and training:** Bachelor's degree. **Annual earnings:** $64,230. **Annual openings:** 17,000. **Job growth through 2012:** 8.0%.

❑ **Computer Hardware Engineers**

Research, design, develop, and test computer hardware and supervise its manufacture and installation. Hardware refers to computer chips, circuit boards, computer systems, and related equipment such as keyboards, modems, and printers. **Skill levels:** *High:* Mathematics, mechanical, science. *Moderate:* Communication, managerial. *Basic:* Artistic, interpersonal. **Education and training:** Bachelor's degree. **Annual earnings:** $81,150. **Annual openings:** 6,000. **Job growth through 2012:** 6.1%.

❑ **Electrical and Electronics Engineers, except Computer**

Design, develop, test, and supervise the manufacture of electrical and electronic equipment. Write performance requirements, develop maintenance schedules, test equipment, solve operating problems, and estimate the time and cost of engineering projects. **Skill levels:** *High:* Mathematics, mechanical, science. *Moderate:* Communication, managerial. *Basic:* Artistic, interpersonal. **Education and training:** Bachelor's degree. **Annual earnings:** $73,548. **Annual openings:** 22,000. **Job growth through 2012:** 5.7%.

❑ **Materials Engineers**

Evaluate materials and develop machinery and processes to manufacture materials for use in products that must meet specialized design and performance specifications. Develop new uses for known materials. **Skill levels:** *High:* Mathematics, mechanical, science. *Moderate:* Communication, managerial. *Basic:* Artistic, interpersonal. **Education and training:**

Bachelor's degree. **Annual earnings:** $67,110. **Annual openings:** 2,000. **Job growth through 2012:** 4.1%.

❏ **Mechanical Engineers**
Perform engineering duties in planning and designing tools, engines, machines, and other mechanically functioning equipment. Oversee installation, operation, maintenance, and repair of such equipment as centralized heat, gas, water, and steam systems. **Skill levels:** *High:* Mathematics, mechanical, science. *Moderate:* Artistic, communication, managerial. *Basic:* Interpersonal. **Education and training:** Bachelor's degree. **Annual earnings:** $66,320. **Annual openings:** 14,000. **Job growth through 2012:** 4.8%.

❏ **Nuclear Engineers**
Conduct research on nuclear engineering problems or apply principles and theory of nuclear science to problems concerned with release, control, and utilization of nuclear energy and nuclear waste disposal. **Skill levels:** *High:* Mathematics, mechanical, science. *Moderate:* Communication, managerial. *Basic:* Artistic, interpersonal. **Education and training:** Bachelor's degree. **Annual earnings:** $84,880. **Annual openings:** 1,000. **Job growth through 2012:** –0.1%.

Industrial and Safety Engineering

❏ **Industrial Engineers, Including Health and Safety**
Design, develop, test, and evaluate integrated systems for managing industrial production processes including human work factors, quality control, inventory control, logistics and material flow, cost analysis, and production coordination. **Skill levels:** *High:* Mathematics, mechanical, science. *Moderate:* Artistic, communication, managerial. *Basic:* Interpersonal. **Education and training:** Bachelor's degree. **Annual earnings:** $64,781. **Annual openings:** 20,000. **Job growth through 2012:** 10.1%.

Engineering Technology

❏ **Drafters**
Prepare technical drawings and plans to serve as visual guidelines for production and construction workers, show the technical details of products and structures, and specify dimensions, materials, and procedures. **Skill levels:** *High:* Artistic, mechanical. *Moderate:* Communication, mathematics. *Basic:* Interpersonal, science. *Not essential:* Managerial. **Education and training:** Postsecondary vocational award. **Annual earnings:** $41,162. **Annual openings:** 28,000. **Job growth through 2012:** 2.8%.

❑ **Engineering Technicians**
Use the principles and theories of science, engineering, and mathematics to solve technical problems in research and development, manufacturing, sales, construction, inspection, and maintenance. **Skill levels:** *High:* Mathematics, mechanical, science. *Moderate:* Communication. *Basic:* Artistic, interpersonal. *Not essential:* Managerial. **Education and training:** Associate degree. **Annual earnings:** $43,685. **Annual openings:** 56,000. **Job growth through 2012:** 10.0%.

❑ **Surveyors, Cartographers, Photogrammetrists, and Surveying Technicians**
Measure and map earth's surface. May establish official land, air space, and water boundaries; provide data relevant to the shape, contour, location, elevation, or dimension of land features; or compile geographic, political, and cultural information. **Skill levels:** *Moderate:* Artistic, communication, interpersonal, mathematics, mechanical, science. *Basic:* Managerial. **Education and training:** Bachelor's degree. **Annual earnings:** $37,155. **Annual openings:** 17,000. **Job growth through 2012:** 14.1%.

16. Transportation, Distribution, and Logistics

Managerial Work in Transportation
❑ **Rail Transportation Occupations**
Drive or operate equipment on railway vehicles, such as trains or subways, to transport passengers and freight; operate railroad equipment such as track switches; or coordinate activities of train crew. **Skill levels:** *High:* Mechanical. *Moderate:* Communication. *Basic:* Interpersonal, managerial, science. *Not essential:* Artistic, mathematics. **Education and training:** Work experience in a related occupation. **Annual earnings:** $47,655. **Annual openings:** 11,000. **Job growth through 2012:** –8.6%.

Air Vehicle Operation
❑ **Aircraft Pilots and Flight Engineers**
Pilot and navigate the flight of aircraft for the transport of cargo or passengers. May instruct people in how to fly aircraft. **Skill levels:** *High:* Communication, interpersonal, managerial, mathematics, science. *Moderate:* Mechanical. *Not essential:* Artistic. **Education and training:** Bachelor's degree. **Annual earnings:** $113,420. **Annual openings:** 8,000. **Job growth through 2012:** 17.7%.

Truck Driving

❑ **Truck Drivers and Driver/Sales Workers**
Drive a truck, tractor-trailer, or van to transport and deliver merchandise. May cover an established territory and also sell or pick up goods. **Skill levels:** *Basic:* Communication, mechanical. *Not essential:* Artistic, interpersonal, managerial, mathematics, science. **Education and training:** Moderate-term on-the-job training. **Annual earnings:** $28,872. **Annual openings:** 585,000. **Job growth through 2012:** 18.4%.

Rail Vehicle Operation

❑ **Rail Transportation Occupations**
Drive or operate equipment on railway vehicles, such as trains or subways, to transport passengers and freight; operate railroad equipment such as track switches; or coordinate activities of train crew. **Skill levels:** *High:* Mechanical. *Moderate:* Communication. *Basic:* Interpersonal, managerial, science. *Not essential:* Artistic, mathematics. **Education and training:** Work experience in a related occupation. **Annual earnings:** $47,655. **Annual openings:** 11,000. **Job growth through 2012:** –8.6%.

Water Vehicle Operation

❑ **Material Moving Occupations**
Use machinery to move construction materials, earth, petroleum products, and other heavy materials, generally over short distances; manually handle freight, stock, or other materials; clean equipment; or feed materials into processing machinery. **Skill levels:** *High:* Mechanical. *Basic:* Communication. *Not essential:* Artistic, interpersonal, managerial, mathematics, science. **Education and training:** Moderate-term on-the-job training. **Annual earnings:** $26,896. **Annual openings:** 930,000. **Job growth through 2012:** –1.5%.

❑ **Water Transportation Occupations**
Operate and maintain deep-sea merchant ships, tugboats, towboats, ferries, dredges, excursion vessels, and other waterborne craft on the oceans, the Great Lakes, rivers, canals, and other waterways, as well as in harbors. **Skill levels:** *High:* Managerial, mechanical. *Moderate:* Communication, mathematics, science. *Basic:* Interpersonal. *Not essential:* Artistic. **Education and training:** Moderate-term on-the-job training. **Annual earnings:** $40,819. **Annual openings:** 8,000. **Job growth through 2012:** 3.4%.

Other Services Requiring Driving

❑ **Bus Drivers**

Drive bus or motor coach, including regular city and intercity routes, charters, and school routes. May assist passengers with baggage. May collect fares or tickets. May assist passengers in boarding or exiting. **Skill levels:** *Basic:* Communication, interpersonal, mechanical. *Not essential:* Artistic, managerial, mathematics, science. **Education and training:** Short-term on-the-job training. **Annual earnings:** $25,248. **Annual openings:** 109,000. **Job growth through 2012:** 16.2%.

❑ **Couriers and Messengers**

Move and distribute information, documents, and small packages for businesses, institutions, and government agencies; pick up and deliver letters, important business documents, or packages that need to be sent or received quickly within a local area. **Skill levels:** *Basic:* Communication, interpersonal, mathematics, mechanical. *Not essential:* Artistic, managerial, science. **Education and training:** Short-term on-the-job training. **Annual earnings:** $20,190. **Annual openings:** 25,000. **Job growth through 2012:** 4.0%.

❑ **Material Recording, Scheduling, Dispatching, and Distributing Occupations**

Coordinate, expedite, and track orders for personnel, materials, and equipment. **Skill levels:** *Basic:* Communication, interpersonal, mathematics, mechanical. *Not essential:* Artistic, managerial, science. **Education and training:** Short-term on-the-job training. **Annual earnings:** $26,930. **Annual openings:** 768,000. **Job growth through 2012:** 0.6%.

❑ **Postal Service Workers**

Deliver mail or perform any combination of tasks in a post office, such as receive letters and parcels; sell postage stamps; fill out and sell money orders; and place mail in pigeon holes of mail rack. **Skill levels:** *Basic:* Communication, interpersonal, managerial, mathematics, mechanical. *Not essential:* Artistic, science. **Education and training:** Short-term on-the-job training. **Annual earnings:** $42,131. **Annual openings:** 43,000. **Job growth through 2012:** –4.3%.

❑ **Taxi Drivers and Chauffeurs**

Drive automobiles, vans, or limousines to transport passengers. May occasionally carry cargo. **Skill levels:** *Basic:* Communication, interpersonal, mechanical. *Not essential:* Artistic, managerial, mathematics, science.

Education and training: Short-term on-the-job training. **Annual earnings:** $19,570. **Annual openings:** 28,000. **Job growth through 2012:** 21.7%.

❏ **Truck Drivers and Driver/Sales Workers**
Drive a truck, tractor-trailer, or van to transport and deliver merchandise. May cover an established territory and also sell or pick up goods. **Skill levels:** *Basic:* Communication, mechanical. *Not essential:* Artistic, interpersonal, managerial, mathematics, science. **Education and training:** Moderate-term on-the-job training. **Annual earnings:** $28,872. **Annual openings:** 585,000. **Job growth through 2012:** 18.4%.

Transportation Support Work

❏ **Cargo and Freight Agents**
Arrange for and track incoming and outgoing cargo and freight shipments in airline, train, or trucking terminals or on shipping docks. **Skill levels:** *Moderate:* Mathematics. *Basic:* Communication, interpersonal, managerial, science. *Not essential:* Artistic, mechanical. **Education and training:** Moderate-term on-the-job training. **Annual earnings:** $34,250. **Annual openings:** 8,000. **Job growth through 2012:** 15.5%.

❏ **Material Recording, Scheduling, Dispatching, and Distributing Occupations**
Coordinate, expedite, and track orders for personnel, materials, and equipment. **Skill levels:** *Basic:* Communication, interpersonal, mathematics, mechanical. *Not essential:* Artistic, managerial, science. **Education and training:** Short-term on-the-job training. **Annual earnings:** $26,930. **Annual openings:** 768,000. **Job growth through 2012:** 0.6%.

❏ **Rail Transportation Occupations**
Drive or operate equipment on railway vehicles, such as trains or subways, to transport passengers and freight; operate railroad equipment such as track switches; or coordinate activities of train crew. **Skill levels:** *High:* Mechanical. *Moderate:* Communication. *Basic:* Interpersonal, managerial, science. *Not essential:* Artistic, mathematics. **Education and training:** Work experience in a related occupation. **Annual earnings:** $47,655. **Annual openings:** 11,000. **Job growth through 2012:** –8.6%.

Go Back and Review the Job Descriptions

Go back to the jobs you checked and read their descriptions to learn more about them. This step will help you eliminate some jobs and identify the relatively few jobs that are *most* interesting to you. Circle or underline the relatively few jobs that interest you most. When you are done, write the five to ten jobs that *most* interest you in the box that follows. Do not eliminate any job that interests you because of its education requirements, skills, or other factors. If it interests you, and you think you would enjoy it, list the job below. You can always eliminate it later.

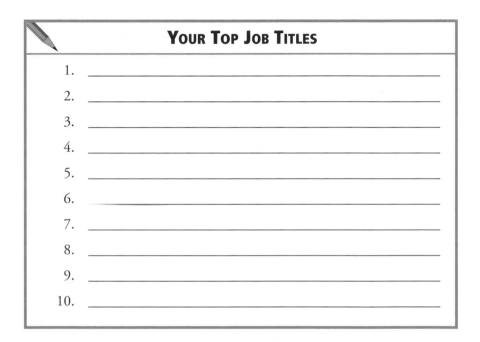

YOUR TOP JOB TITLES

1. _____

2. _____

3. _____

4. _____

5. _____

6. _____

7. _____

8. _____

9. _____

10. _____

You will need to learn more about some of the jobs on your list before making a final decision. Some may require additional training or education, for example.

The Job Exploration Worksheet in Appendix A can help you do more research on specific jobs as needed. In Chapter 8, you will combine your top job titles with your career preferences from earlier chapters to create your career focus.

More About the Data in the Job Descriptions

Here are more details on the information in the job descriptions.

Understanding the Skill Levels

Seven personal skill levels are listed for each job description and rated as high, moderate, basic, or not essential. High-skill levels are essential to the job. Moderate-skill levels are somewhat essential. Basic-level skills are mildly essential to the job. The skill information was derived from the *Occupational Outlook Quarterly,* which is published by the U.S. Department of Labor.

Occupations are classified based on how frequently skills are used and by what level of skill is usually needed. The ratings in the job descriptions are averages, based on tasks that are most commonly performed by the majority of workers in each occupation. For example, a high level of math skills is not required for some computer programmers, such as those who work on user interfaces, but high-level math skills are required for most computer programmers—including some who prepare physics simulations that require calculus. Based on the level of skills that most of these workers need, mathematics ability is rated as essential for computer programmers. In another example, managerial skills are rated as being of basic importance for construction and building inspectors, who are primarily independent but sometimes must advise other workers.

Here is some general information about the skills in the job descriptions.

- **Artistic skills.** Occupations that require artistic skills tap workers' sense of what is beautiful or well designed.

- **Communication skills.** Nearly all workers need communication skills. But the job descriptions show which occupations require more complex levels of English language comprehension.

- **Interpersonal skills.** Interpersonal skills refer to workers' ability to interact effectively with other people and to be persuasive.

- **Managerial skills.** Managerial skills include the ability to organize, direct, and instruct other workers.

- **Mathematics skills.** Mathematics skills refer to more advanced ability than the core math skills required in nearly all jobs. The rating shows either the frequency or complexity of the skill required.

- **Mechanical skills.** Mechanical skills include a broad range of abilities, such as installation, maintenance, troubleshooting, and quality control analysis.

- **Science skills.** Basic science skills include an ability to apply some scientific theories and to communicate about science. Moderate science skills involve theoretical scientific knowledge, and high-level science skills involve in-depth practical knowledge.

Understanding the Education Levels

This "education and training" entry in the job descriptions gives you information on the education and training typically required for entry into the job. Some jobs that interest you may require more training or education than you have or want to consider getting. Don't eliminate these too quickly! If a job really interests you, learn more about it. If you really want to do that kind of work, you can often find ways to get the training or education needed.

Here is more information on the education and training levels used in the job descriptions:

- **First professional degree.** Typically requires a minimum of two years of education beyond the bachelor's degree and frequently requires three years.

- **Doctoral degree.** Normally requires two or more years of full-time academic work beyond the bachelor's degree.

- **Master's degree.** Usually requires one to two years of full-time study beyond the bachelor's degree.

- **Work experience plus degree.** Bachelor's degree plus related work experience. Jobs requiring this education level are often management-related and require some experience in a related nonmanagerial position.

- **Bachelor's degree.** A four-year academic program beyond high school.

- **Associate degree.** A two-year academic program beyond high school.

- **Postsecondary vocational award.** Specific job-related training lasting from several months to several years. Some high schools provide substantial vocational training, although most is obtained after high school.

- **Work experience in a related occupation.** Experience in a related job.

- **Long-term on-the-job training.** More than one year of on-the-job training or a combination of training and formal classroom instruction.

- **Moderate-term on-the-job training.** One to twelve months of on-the-job training.

- **Short-term on-the-job training.** Up to one month of on-the-job training.

Understanding Earnings, Openings, and Job Growth Information

The average wage for all jobs is $29,000. The average growth for all jobs is 14.8 percent through 2012.

To create the data in the job descriptions, we linked the *Occupational Outlook Handbook* jobs to the latest information on wages, employment outlook, and requirements for education or training from the U.S. Department of Labor. In cases where an *OOH* job is linked to more than one job for which data is gathered (for example, Writers and Editors), we calculated a weighted average for wages and job growth and summed the figures for job openings. When the linked jobs had differing levels of required education or training, we used the level of the job with the most workers or, when those numbers were equal, we used the higher level.

What's Next?

Now that you have identified the job titles that interest you most and the other factors important to you in a career, the next chapter helps you look at the industries you may enjoy.

Key Points: Chapter 6

- Focusing on job titles may cause you to overlook factors that are important for career success.

- Accurate information about specific jobs is a key part of career planning.

- The jobs described in this chapter appear in a longer form in the *Occupational Outlook Handbook,* a book published every two years by the U.S. Department of Labor and available from JIST.

Chapter 7

Identify Industries That Interest You

While most people understand the advantage of wanting a certain type of job rather than "any" job, they often overlook the importance of considering various industries. Yet what industry you work in is often as important as what job you choose. Why? There are various reasons, but here are the primary ones:

- **Some industries pay better.** Let's say you want to manage a warehouse operation or work in an office support position. If so, it might help you to know that you are more likely to be paid better in the drug manufacturing industry than in the department store or grocery store industries. You have the same basic job, doing the same basic sorts of things, but one industry pays better. That could end up being a very important difference to you over time.

- **Some industries present more risk or less stability.** Some industries routinely hire more people when the economy is strong and lay off people when it is weak. Other industries tend to be more stable in their employment and less affected by short-term business cycles. Some industries are growing rapidly, others are declining, and many are changing as a result of technology or other forces. If it is important for you to work in a stable situation where you are less likely to be laid off, then select a more stable industry.

- **Some industries will be more fun for you.** Some industries will appeal to you more for a variety of reasons. You could be interested based on your interests, values, previous training or education, or a variety of other factors. Selecting an industry that appeals to you could be as important to you as the job you do.

Some Background on Industry Growth

The data that follows shows the projected growth in number of people employed in various industries in the ten-year period ending 2012.

The table also gives you information on the percent of the workforce within each industry and industry group.

While this is a lot of data to absorb, it relates to some things you should consider in making your career plans. As you look at the data, notice that it is organized into two major groups consisting of "goods-producing industries" and "service-providing industries." Within these two major groups are subgroups of related industries. I'll note some trends and make observations following the data table.

Projected Growth by Industry		
Industry	Percent of Workforce Employed	Percent Growth in Employment
ALL INDUSTRIES	100	16.3
GOODS-PRODUCING INDUSTRIES	18.0	3.2
Natural resources and mining	1.4	−4.9
Agriculture, forestry, fishing, and hunting	0.9	−1.9
Oil and gas extraction	0.1	−27.8
Mining	0.2	−15.0
Construction	5.1	15.1
Manufacturing	11.6	−1.0
Aerospace product and parts manufacturing	0.4	−17.6
Apparel manufacturing	0.3	−68.6
Chemical manufacturing, except drugs	0.5	−16.7
Computer and electronic product manufacturing	1.1	12.4
Food manufacturing	1.2	4.7
Motor vehicle and parts manufacturing	0.9	2.6
Pharmaceutical and medicine manufacturing	0.2	23.2
Printing	0.5	3.3
Steel manufacturing	0.1	−20.0
Textile mills and products	0.4	−31.0
SERVICE-PROVIDING INDUSTRIES	82.0	19.2
Trade, transportation, and utilities	19.3	14.1
Automobile dealers	0.9	12.6

Industry	Percent of Workforce Employed	Percent Growth in Employment
Clothing, accessory, and general merchandise stores	3.1	8.3
Grocery stores	1.9	5.4
Wholesale trade	4.3	11.3
Air transportation	0.4	12.0
Truck transportation and warehousing	1.4	22.7
Utilities	0.5	−5.7
Information	**2.6**	**18.5**
Broadcasting	0.3	8.5
Motion picture and video industries	0.3	31.1
Publishing, except software	0.5	−1.5
Software publishers	0.2	67.9
Telecommunications	0.9	6.7
Financial activities	**4.4**	**10.1**
Banking	1.3	6.4
Insurance	1.7	7.5
Securities, commodities, and other investments	0.6	15.5
Personal and business services	**12.1**	**30.4**
Advertising and public relations services	0.3	18.9
Computer systems design and related services	0.9	54.6
Employment services	2.5	54.3
Management, scientific, and technical consulting services	0.6	55.4
Education and health services	**19.7**	**26.4**
Child day care services	0.6	43.1
Educational services	9.5	19.9
Health services	9.5	28.0
Social assistance, except child day care	1.0	47.1
Leisure and hospitality	**9.0**	**17.8**
Arts, entertainment, and recreation	1.3	28.0
Food services and drinking places	6.4	15.9
Hotels and other accommodations	1.3	16.9

(continued)

(continued)

Industry	Percent of Workforce Employed	Percent Growth in Employment
Public administration	7.4	8.3
Federal government, excluding the postal service	1.5	2.6
State and local government, except education and health	5.9	9.7

Note: May not add to totals due to smaller industries not listed.

This data shows some important things to consider in your career planning. Here are some highlights.

Goods-producing industries. These industries manufacture, grow, build, or mine something. Goods-producing industries are projected to increase, although not as rapidly as the average for all industries. Jobs that are in the "manufacturing" industry group are projected to decrease. Reasons for decline are sometimes related to technological improvements that automate functions and reduce the need for workers. Other industries, such as apparel manufacturing, are projected to have fewer jobs as a result of foreign competition. Construction and pharmaceutical and medicine manufacturing will see the biggest increases.

> **Tip:** *Health services and educational services—the two largest industries—will account for the most new jobs through 2012.*

Service-providing industries. More than 80 percent of all employment is in this major sector, and this is where much of the future growth is projected to occur. Only two industry groups are expected to decline: utilities and publishing (except software). All other industries in this large group are expected to increase their employment. As you look through the list, note that some industries are growing much more rapidly than average. Software publishers (67.9 percent); management, scientific, and technical consulting services (55.4 percent); computer systems design and related services (54.6 percent); and employment services (54.3 percent) are among the most rapidly growing industries.

Service-Providing Industries Have Accounted for Virtually All Growth

While recent data on the increase or decline in industries or occupations seem minor, the information can be quite significant over a long period. Before the industrial revolution, for example, more than 50 percent of the workforce in this country worked on farms. Now, less than 1 percent of our workforce is involved in farming, yet we have more and better food than ever and enough left over to export. Just as with farming, many believe that more efficient factories and improved technologies result in more and better goods being produced by fewer workers. If so, this trend would be similar to what became of all the farm workers: Improved technologies reduced the percent of the workforce required to create what we need. While this is a bit oversimplified, the fact is that most of the growth in employment over recent decades has been in the services-providing industries and not in the goods-producing industries.

Opportunities will remain in all industries, including manufacturing, agriculture, and other slow-growth or no-growth industries. This is a very large country, and even small industries that are declining will have openings for well-trained people. What is clear, however, is that this is not your grandfather's economy. Almost all of the net new jobs have been created outside of manufacturing, and this trend is likely to increase.

Most Job Opportunities Are with Small Employers

Large employers employ a lower percentage of workers than in the past. For example, the FORTUNE 500, consisting of the country's 500 largest employers, decreased the number of people they employed by more than 25 percent between 1980 and the mid 1990s, and the number of people they employ continues to decline. This dramatic decrease occurred during a time when millions of new jobs were being created. Where did all those new jobs come from? Small employers.

The data that follows comes from the U.S. Department of Labor's Bulletin 2541. It shows the percent of all workers employed in organizations of different sizes. This data shows that smaller employers, those with 249 or fewer workers, now employ more than 70 percent of the workforce.

(continued)

(continued)

Employment by Size of Establishment

Establishment Size by Number of Workers Employed	Percent of All Workers Employed
1 to 4	5.9
5 to 9	8.1
10 to 19	10.7
20 to 49	16.3
50 to 99	12.8
100 to 249	16.4
250 to 499	9.6
500 to 999	7.2
1,000 or more	13.2

An economist named David Burch researched the job-generating ability of various sized businesses. His conclusion was that the smallest companies, those with 20 or fewer employees, are responsible for creating as many as 80 percent of the net new jobs that are added to our economy.

While larger employers will remain an important source of employment, small businesses are more important to our economy than ever before. Smaller employers cannot be ignored as a major source of employment opportunities.

Review 42 Major Industries

This section contains a list of 42 major industries that cover most of the labor market. Complete the checklist that follows to give you some ideas about what industries you should consider more closely.

CHECKLIST OF INDUSTRIES TO CONSIDER IN MORE DETAIL

The first column lists the industry. The next three columns allow you to decide how interested you are in working in that industry or in learning more about it. If an industry does not interest you at all, put a check mark in the "No Interest" column. If that industry interests

---

you somewhat or you are not sure, put a check mark in the "Somewhat Interested" column. It that industry seems very interesting to you, put a check mark in the "Very Interested" column.

Industry to Consider	No Interest	Somewhat Interested	Very Interested
GOODS-PRODUCING INDUSTRIES			
Natural resources and mining			
Agriculture, forestry, fishing, and hunting			
Oil and gas extraction			
Mining			
Construction			
Manufacturing			
Aerospace product and parts manufacturing			
Apparel manufacturing			
Chemical manufacturing, except drugs			
Computer and electronic product manufacturing			
Food manufacturing			
Motor vehicle and parts manufacturing			
Pharmaceutical and medicine manufacturing			
Printing			
Steel manufacturing			
Textile mills and products			
SERVICE-PROVIDING INDUSTRIES			
Trade, transportation, and utilities			
Automobile dealers			
Clothing, accessory, and general merchandise stores			
Grocery stores			
Wholesale trade			
Air transportation			
Truck transportation and warehousing			
Utilities			

(continued)

(continued)

Industry to Consider	No Interest	Somewhat Interested	Very Interested
Information			
Broadcasting			
Motion picture and video industries			
Publishing, except software			
Software publishers			
Telecommunications			
Financial activities			
Banking			
Insurance			
Securities, commodities, and other investments			
Personal and business services			
Advertising and public relations services			
Computer systems design and related services			
Employment services			
Management, scientific, and technical consulting services			
Education and health services			
Child day care services			
Educational services			
Health services			
Social assistance, except child day care			
Leisure and hospitality			
Arts, entertainment, and recreation			
Food services and drinking places			
Hotels and other accommodations			
Public administration			
Federal government, excluding the postal service			
State and local government, except education and health			

Write in below other industries that interest you that are not in the checklist above:

_____

Now identify the industries you most want to learn about. Review the checklist and select the five industries that you most want to consider in your ideal career and write them below.

1. _____

_____

2. _____

_____

3. _____

_____

4. _____

_____

5. _____

_____

Learn More About Targeted Industries

Details on the industries in the checklist you completed are tracked by the U.S. Department of Labor. Helpful descriptions for these industries appear in a government publication titled *Career Guide to Industries,* which is published every two years. A version of this book that is readily available in bookstores and libraries is called *40 Best Fields for Your Career.* It is published by JIST and can be ordered from www.jist.com. You can also find the industry descriptions at www.bls.gov under the "Publications" section.

The industry descriptions in these resources include the following information:

- Significant points
- Nature of the industry
- Working conditions
- Employment
- Occupations in the industry
- Training and advancement

- Earnings
- Outlook
- Sources of additional information

If you decide to do more industry research later, here are some steps you can take to get the most out of these industry descriptions:

- **Mark them up.** Circle or underline anything that is particularly important to you, like the pay rates, skills, education, or training required.

- **Include important requirements in your interviews and resume.** Later, when you are looking for a job in this industry, emphasize the points you underlined that are also important to employers. For example, do you have the skills that this industry requires? Do you have related interests, experience, or education? Can you mention important trends to indicate your knowledge of the industry?

- **Pay particular attention to the related jobs.** While some jobs are found in most industries (such as accountants, administrative support, and clerical workers), industry-related jobs are listed at the end of the industry descriptions in the publications I just mentioned.

- **Consider pay, growth, and other factors.** I mentioned earlier that some industries pay better than others. So consider working in an industry that pays better than average, particularly if you find it of interest. You should also, of course, consider other factors such as industry growth and stability. For example, government jobs tend to be more stable than jobs in industries that are more sensitive to changes in the economy.

Key Points: Chapter 7

- The industry you work in is often as important as what job you choose because of pay, stability, your interest in it, and other factors.

- More than 80 percent of all employment is in the service-providing sector, and this is where much of the future growth is projected to occur.

- Smaller employers, those with 249 or fewer workers, employ more than 70 percent of the workforce.

- Use standard reference sources to learn more about industries that interest you most.

Chapter 8

Overnight Career Choice Matrix and Action Plan

In previous chapters, I've given you a variety of information and advice to help you define what you want in your ideal job. In this chapter, I help you put it all together so that you can find your career focus.

Keep in mind, however, that career planning is an imperfect process that may require you to ultimately compromise and take some chances. Although being completely satisfied with anything is not part of the human condition, this chapter pulls together a combination of things to increase the possibility of selecting a job that fits you well.

I've suggested previously that you should combine a job with the type of organization or industry in which you have an interest. For example, if you have experience or training in accounting and love airplanes, you might consider looking for an accounting-related position in the aircraft manufacturing industry, an agency monitoring airline safety, or in an industry that provides materials or services to the aircraft industry. There are many other possibilities you may think of if you combined those three elements of job, industry/organization type, and interest.

You can do the same thing with the ideal job factors you identified earlier in this book. For example, if you have experience in marketing and love to cook in your free time, it may make sense for you to look for a position in a food or restaurant-related industry. Combining a type of job with an industry that interests you can make a lot of sense.

In a similar way, you can also combine a type of job with several or all of the factors important in an ideal job. You considered these factors in Chapters 2 through 5, and they include

1. Skills and abilities

2. Interests

3. Personal values

4. Preferred earnings

5. Level of responsibility

6. Location

7. Special knowledge

8. Work environment

9. Types of people you like to work with or for

Summarize the Characteristics of Your Ideal Career

This section helps you gather your thoughts and narrow down your ideal career. Answer each question by including those things you identified as being most important to you in the activities you worked through earlier in this book. In some cases, such as the question about skills, you may need to review previous chapters to refresh your memory.

Use this worksheet to clarify the characteristics of a career choice that is a good match for you in a variety of ways. Answer each question by including only those two or three things that are most important to you.

MY IDEAL CAREER

1. What skills or abilities do you most want to use or include in your career? Refer to Chapter 2 if needed.

   Adaptive skills or abilities:

   _____

   _____

   _____

   Transferable skills or abilities:

   _____

   _____

   _____

Job-related skills or abilities:

_____

_____

_____

2. What sorts of things interest you that you may want to include or pursue in your ideal career? Refer to Chapter 3 if needed.

_____

_____

_____

_____

3. What values are particularly important for you to include or pursue in your ideal career? Refer to Chapter 4 if needed.

_____

_____

_____

4. What range of earnings do you expect or prefer? Refer to Chapter 5 if needed.

_____

5. What level of responsibility would you prefer in your work? Refer to Chapter 5 if needed.

_____

_____

6. What location or geographic characteristics would you prefer? Refer to Chapter 5 if needed.

_____

_____

(continued)

(continued)

7. What special knowledge or interests would you like to use or pursue in your ideal career? Refer to Chapter 5 if needed.

_____

_____

8. What type of work environment do you prefer? Refer to Chapter 5 if needed.

_____

_____

9. What types of people would you prefer to work with or for? Refer to Chapter 5 if needed.

_____

_____

THE THREE MOST IMPORTANT THINGS TO INCLUDE IN MY IDEAL CAREER

After you have completed the preceding worksheet, select the three and only three things that are *most* important to include in your ideal career. Write those three things below.

1. _____

2. _____

3. _____

Put Your Ideal Career Characteristics into Graphic Form with the Career Wheel

This optional activity takes the factors you listed in the previous section and puts them into graphic form. For some people, a graphic form can help them better remember and use the information. Fill in the career wheel with your responses.

My ideal job would include the following:

The Career Wheel

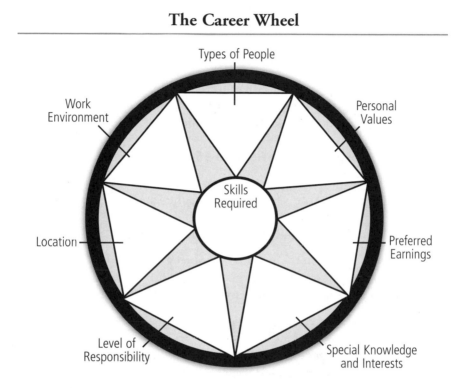

Brainstorm Combinations with the Overnight Career Choice Matrix

The Overnight Career Choice Matrix that follows will help you brainstorm creative combinations of job title, industry, and the ideal job factors you identified earlier.

Tip: *Be creative with the Overnight Career Choice Matrix. Don't be afraid to brainstorm and take some chances—it's all just on paper at this point.*

OVERNIGHT CAREER CHOICE MATRIX

The Overnight Career Choice Matrix has three columns and six rows. You can make your own matrix on separate sheets of paper and include more rows and columns that combine more factors. Use the matrix to come up with interesting and creative jobs possibilities.

Step 1: Work Groups or Job Titles

Chapter 6 helped you select work groups and job titles that interest you. In the top row of the matrix, write three specific work group names or job titles that interest you the most.

Step 2: Industries and Ideal Job Factors

Down the left side of the matrix are spaces for you to write. The first three rows provide spaces for you to write the names of industries from Chapter 7 that interest you. Write the name of one industry in each space provided in the first three rows of the matrix.

Next, write three factors you selected as being most important to include in your next job. Write one most important factor in the remaining three rows on the Overnight Career Choice Matrix.

Step 3: Be Creative

Now it is time to get creative. Let's say you wrote "Public Relations Specialist" as a job title and "Agriculture" as a top industry (because you grew up on a farm and know a lot about this). The box in the upper-left corner is where these two items intersect. In that box, write any possible jobs that might combine the job of Public Relations Specialist in the Agriculture industry. Can you think of anything? A few obvious combinations might occur to you, like "PR for an agricultural chemical company" or "PR for a government ag program" as well as some that may not be so obvious. Write anything that occurs to you in that box, even if it seems unrealistic or silly.

Then go to the next box, either down or across (whatever makes more sense to you), and repeat the process for a new combination of factors to consider. For example, let's say you wrote "cross-country bicycle racing" in the fourth row down because that is something you love to do in your free time. Can you think of any jobs that would combine Public Relations Specialist with bicycle racing? Yep, I can: "PR for a bicycle manufacturer or parts supplier" and "promoting races" and "building interest in cycling by working for a bicycle racing association" for just a few ideas.

Repeat this same process for each and every box on your Overnight Career Choice Matrix, writing any job ideas that combine the two elements that intersect in each box.

Overnight Career Choice Matrix

	Work Group or Job Title	Work Group or Job Title	Work Group or Job Title
Top Industry			
Top Industry			
Top Industry			
Ideal Job Factor			
Ideal Job Factor			
Ideal Job Factor			

(continued)

(continued)

Step 4: Identify the Combinations That Make the Most Sense to You

Some job combinations won't make much sense or will not seem interesting or practical to you. This is your matrix, so ignore those and circle the ones that make sense to you as possible ideal careers. Remember that you can use additional sheets of paper if needed.

Some of the combinations may seem unreasonably difficult to achieve or to find. But, if a combination interests you, you might be surprised at how well you might be received by an employer who needs someone with that odd combination of interests. For example, if you were to enter "amateur bicycle racing association" in your Web browser, you will find a variety of interesting Web sites of organizations and businesses that are very much involved in this sort of activity. Among them is www.usacycling.org, a site that links to bicycle-racing clubs around the world, bicycle racing parts suppliers, and other related sites.

Find the right people in these settings, and many of them will be happy to help you. Some will give you job leads, some will teach you about what they do and where someone like you might fit in the field, many will accept e-mail and a resume from you, and a few will be willing to interview you.

If you want a career having to do with bicycle racing in some way (or in a variety of other improbable combinations of things that interest you), there are real opportunities. And, if you think about it, if you were an employer in the bicycle racing industry who needed someone with public relations, accounting, warehousing, or sales experience, wouldn't you rather hire someone who loves bicycle racing? Yes, you would, and that will be your competitive edge, if you seek the right career for the right reasons.

Your Ideal Job Definition

In the spaces that follow, write your definition of your ideal job. Refer to the information you summarized in this chapter as needed.

My ideal career is as a _____ in the
(job title)

_____industry,
(industry)

using my _____ skills and back
(key skills and special knowledge)

ground. My _____
(key insterests)

interests and _____ skills make well-
(other skills)

qualified for this career. As part of this career, I would like to

_____. I would enjoy a
(key values)

_____ work environment in
(preferred work environment)

_____. I would like to have
(preferred geographic location/area)

_____ responsibility and work with
(level of responsibility)

_____ people. I would like to earn at least
(types of coworkers)

_____.
(salary)

The activities you just completed help you clearly define the preferred
characteristics of your ideal career. Pursuing a career that is in major conflict with one or more of these factors can lead to job failure or unhappiness. So be clear about what you would prefer in your career focus, even if
it changes in the future.

Your Overnight Career Choice Action Plan

Now that you have assembled the components of your ideal career, your
task is to decide the next step.

Find Your Ideal Job

For many people, the next step is finding a
job that comes as close as possible to meeting
their ideal career criteria. If you conduct a
creative job search, you won't be looking for *a*
job but for the *right* job. Of course, you may

> **Tip:** *Part of the search
> for your ideal job is
> using a clear job objec-
> tive on your resumes
> and applications. The
> next chapter helps you
> with that task.*

need to make some compromise between the ideal and what you accept. But the closer you can come to finding a job that meets your preferences, the better that job will be for you.

After completing this book, you may realize that your current job can become your ideal job—or at least more acceptable—with a few changes. For example, would a promotion or a transfer make your current position more ideal for you? If you took on added responsibility, would your job become more interesting to you? Consider these and similar points when deciding your next move.

Pursue More Education or Training

Maybe your ideal job requires more education or training than you have. While it may seem like a huge or even impossible task to go back to school, break this goal into steps or consider it from another point of view.

Suppose, for example, that you want to be a recreational therapist, which combines your skill in art with your interest in social services and health. Within 60 days, your goal might be to find a source of schooling to prepare you for the occupation and to learn about loans and financing options. That might involve some library or Internet research as well as visits to schools. A one-year goal may be to be enrolled in a school, and a two-year goal may be to continue schooling full-time and to get a part-time job related to your interest to pay the bills. Keep at it and in a few years you will be a recreational therapist.

Or, perhaps, you would like to be a librarian but are not interested in or able to pursue a master's degree. After researching related jobs, you may decide to become a library technician instead.

The Cost of Education and Training

Don't be discouraged if you can't afford the expense of more education. Remember that there are many sources of financial aid, scholarships, loans, and grants. One place to start your research is www.studentaid.ed.gov.

Options to consider for additional training include the following:

- Learn a trade or job while you work, through on-the-job training and work experience.

- Enroll in an apprenticeship or other program that combines on-the-job training with classroom instruction.

- Attend a vocational or technical school to learn job skills such as medical technology, computer repair, auto mechanics, and office skills.

- Participate in accredited online learning programs, accelerated programs, or night classes. Investigate local programs in your area, ask people you know for program recommendations, and consult your librarian for good information sources for more research.

- Get training and work experience in the armed forces.

- Pursue related volunteer work, internships, informal self-study, and related leisure activities to develop job skills.

Take Interim Steps

What if you can't change jobs right now? Perhaps, for example, family or other commitments prevent you from pursuing your ideal career. As noted above, start taking small steps toward your chosen career.

Perhaps you can job shadow someone in the field, do informational interviews to learn more about related careers, do related volunteer or part-time work, and join relevant professional associations. Subscribe to industry publications, read books and Internet sites about the career and the field, and attend related trade shows and other events. These experiences will give you valuable experience, knowledge, and contacts for your future career.

Deciding to do something next—even if it is not your ideal job—is better than doing nothing.

Do More Career Research

You may decide that you need more information about your ideal career, whether on the skills required, the training needed, or other factors. Many resources, including books, videos, professional associations, other people, and online information, can help you. See the appendix for recommended career information resources.

Key Points: Chapter 8

- Career planning is an imperfect process that may require you to ultimately compromise and take some chances.

- You might be surprised at how well your combination of interests, skills, values, and other characteristics will be received by an employer.

- After formulating your ideal career definition, your next steps may include finding a job that matches it, pursuing more education or training, or taking interim steps to achieve your goal.

- Plan to do something specific, soon, to move you toward your goal. Write down some tasks and put time lines on them. For example, research education options over the next 30 days. Or spend four hours a week contacting people in the industries identified in your matrix and asking them for interviews. Write down what you could accomplish by three months, six months, one year, and two years. The important thing is to set a goal and get started.

Chapter 9

Write Your Job Objective

This chapter is more about preparing for the job search than exploring career options. I've written job search books too, so if looking for a good job is in your future, I suggest you learn more about the process from one of my books or other resources.

Many job seekers are not at all clear about what sort of job they want, or why they want it. This book helps bring clarity to what you want to do. This chapter helps you clearly communicate your career choice in a format most employers will value.

For example, your resume needs to clearly answer the employer's question, "Who are you and what can you do for me?" It's difficult to write a job objective that does not exclude you from jobs you would consider yet does not sound as if you are willing to do just about anything. Including a clear, focused job objective is quite helpful to people reading your resume.

Avoid a Self-Centered, "Gimme" Approach

I see many job objectives that emphasize what the person *wants* but that don't provide information on what the person *can do*. For example, an objective that says "Interested in a position that allows me to be creative and offers adequate pay and advancement opportunities" is *not* a good objective at all. Who cares? This objective (a real one that someone actually wrote) displays a self-centered, "gimme" approach that turns off most employers.

Note: *While the language about what* you *want in a job is part of your ideal career definition, it's not something to share completely with employers. When you look for a job, start researching organizations, and begin interviewing, you can use the information you learn about an employer to see if the job fits your other ideal-career criteria.*

Sample Job Objectives

Look through the following examples of simple but useful job objectives. Most provide some information on the type of job the person is seeking, as well as the skills he or she offers. The best ones avoid a narrow job title and keep options open to a wide variety of possibilities within a range of appropriate jobs.

Sample Job Objectives

- A responsible general office position in a busy, medium-sized organization.

- A management position in the warehousing industry. Position should require supervisory, problem-solving, and organizational skills.

- Computer programming and/or systems analysis. Prefer an accounting-oriented emphasis and a solutions-oriented organization.

- Medical assistant or secretary in a physician's office, hospital, or other health services environment.

- Responsible position requiring skills in public relations, writing, and reporting.

- An aggressive and success-oriented professional, seeking a sales position offering both challenge and growth.

- Desire position in the office management, administrative support, or clerical area. Position should require flexibility, good organizational skills, and an ability to handle people.

If you are custom-writing your resume for a specific position, you can cleverly say something like "To obtain a position as (insert position title being sought here) with the (insert employer name here)."

Five Tips for Writing a Good Job Objective

The job objective you write should fit your career focus. But here are some general things to consider when you write it.

1. **Avoid job titles.** Job titles such as "receptionist" or "marketing analyst" can involve very different activities in different organizations. If your resume says your objective is to be a receptionist, you will probably not be considered for such jobs as "office manager" or "marketing assistant," even though you could do them. For this reason, it is best to use broad categories of jobs rather than specific titles, so that you

can be considered for a wide variety of positions related to the skills you have. For example, instead of "receptionist," you could say "responsible office-management or clerical position," if that's what you would really consider and are qualified for.

2. **Define a "bracket of responsibility" to include the potential for upward mobility.** Although you might be willing to accept a variety of jobs related to your skills, you should definitely include jobs that require higher levels of responsibility and pay. The example above would allow the candidate to be considered for an office-management position as well as for office support and clerical jobs. In effect, you should define a "bracket of responsibility" in your objective that includes the range of jobs you are willing to accept. This bracket should include the lower range of jobs you would consider, as well as those that require higher levels of responsibility, up to and including the most responsible job you think you could handle. Even if you have not been given those higher levels of responsibility in the past, many employers will consider you for them if you have the skills to handle them.

3. **Include your most important skills.** What are the most important skills needed for the job you want? Include one or more of these in your job objective statement. The implication is that if you are looking for a job that *requires* "organizational skills," then you must have those skills. Of course, your interview (and resume or job application) should give evidence that you have those skills through specific examples.

4. **Include specifics only if they really matter to you.** If you have substantial experience in a particular industry (such as "computer-controlled machine tools") or you have a narrow, specific objective that you *really* want (such as "art therapist with the mentally handicapped"), it's okay to say so. But you should realize that narrowing your alternatives might

> **Tip:** *If you are writing a chronological resume, you may wish to include a "summary," "profile," or other introductory section instead of an objective. If you're writing a skills/functional resume, a job objective statement becomes more important because the job you want is less obvious on your resume.*
>
> *A chronological resume lists your work experience in order, starting with the most recent experience. A skills/functional resume organizes your experience by types of skills and is better to use if your work experience has gaps or is diverse.*

175

keep you from being considered for other jobs for which you qualify. Still, if that's what you want, it's worth pursuing. I would, however, encourage you to have a second, more general objective ready, just in case.

5. **Be clear about the job you want.** While this book has helped you find your career focus, I encourage you to read more-detailed descriptions of your target career. The descriptions will contain skills to emphasize on your resume and in interviews. The *Occupational Outlook Handbook,* created by the U.S. Department of Labor, contains full narratives on the 275 jobs briefly described in Chapter 6. I recommend it as a good source of information. You can find this book in library reference sections and bookstores, as well as on the Web at www.careeroink.com or the Department of Labor's Web site at www.bls.gov/oco/home.htm. JIST sells a reasonably priced reprint of the *OOH* at www.jist.com or 1-800-648-JIST.

Construct Your Job Objective

Use the following worksheet to help you construct an effective and accurate job objective statement for your resume.

MY JOB OBJECTIVE

Complete each of the following items. When you're done, you'll have a better idea of what to include in your resume's job objective statement.

1. **What sort of position, title, and area of specialization do you want?** Write the type of job you want, just as you might explain it to someone you know.

   _____

   _____

   _____

2. **Define your bracket of responsibility.** Describe the range of jobs you would accept, from the minimum up to those you think you could handle if you were given the chance.

_____

_____

_____

3. **Name the key skills you have that are important in this job.**
Describe the two or three key skills that are particularly
important for success in the job that you are seeking. Select
one or more of these that you are strong in and that you enjoy
using. Write it (or them) here.

_____

_____

_____

4. **Name specific areas of expertise or strong interests that you
want to use in your next job.** If you have substantial interest,
experience, or training in a specific area and want to include it
in your job objective (remembering that it might limit your
options), write it here.

_____

_____

_____

5. **What else is important to you?** Is there anything else you
want to include in your job objective? This could be a value
that is particularly important to you such as "a position that
allows me to help families," "employment in an aggressive and
results-oriented organization," or "a small- to mid-size business."

_____

_____

_____

Finalize Your Job Objective

Most employers are impressed by candidates who are very clear about the jobs they want and why they want them. A good job objective may help to keep your resume out of the trash bin. Few interviews end well unless the interviewer is convinced that you really want the job and have the skills to do it. For that reason it is essential to have a clear job objective.

Using your answers from the preceding worksheet, write you job objective here. You can fine-tune it later if needed.

> **Tip:** *Although a simple chronological resume does not require a career objective, a skills resume does. Without a reasonably clear job objective, it is not possible to select and organize the key skills you have to support that objective.*

Job objective: _____

_____

_____

_____

_____

_____

Now that you have your career focus and your job objective, you can go out and get interviews for jobs that closely approximate what you want. In interviews, support your interest in the job by presenting the skills and experiences you have and the advantages you present over other candidates. It sounds simple enough—and it can be—as long as you are clear about what job you want to do and are well organized about finding it.

A Few Final Comments

I hope you have found this book helpful. I tried to make it short, easy to use, and quick to complete. You really can complete all of the book in one day and have a clearer career objective overnight.

But career and life planning is never really complete, since we change over time. We gain more experience, learn more about what we do and do not want, shed or gain responsibilities, get bored and develop new interests. So whatever makes sense for you today may change over time. Our lives interact with our careers; it is simply the way things are.

So do "sleep" overnight on whatever you have learned about career planning from this book today. Understand that it is not important to know precisely what you want to do forever. Instead, think about what is important to you *now* and ask yourself, "What do I want to do next?" as a way of setting your course for the future.

I wish you well in your career and your life.

Key Points: Chapter 9

- Write a job objective from an employer's point of view: what sorts of things can you do, and what skills, experience, and other assets do you offer? Writing a brief and well-done job objective for your resume will help you later in interviews and the job search.

- Be careful to not write a job objective with a self-centered, "gimme" approach, which turns off most employers.

- Five tips for writing your job objective include avoid job titles, define a "bracket of responsibility," include your most important skills, include specifics only if they really matter to you, and be clear about the job you want.

Job Exploration Worksheet

This worksheet helps you collect additional information on specific jobs. Make one photocopy of the worksheet for each job title you research. Start by getting more information on the jobs you listed in "Your Top Job Titles" in Chapter 6. Use the reference sources listed elsewhere in this book or in Appendix B.

JOB EXPLORATION WORKSHEET

Basic Information on This Job

Job title _____

Interest area _____

Source(s) of information used to research this job _____

_____

More Information on This Job

What do people in this job do? _____

_____

_____

_____

_____

_____

Key skills and abilities this job requires _____

_____

_____

Training, education, other qualifications needed _____

_____

Projected growth rate _____

Average earnings (national) _____

Working conditions _____

_____

Level of responsibility _____

_____

Does this job incorporate your top interests?_____

_____

Is this job likely to take advantage of your special knowledge? _____

_____

Is this job likely to include your most important values? _____

_____

Types of coworkers that you will most likely have on this job _____

_____

Is this job most likely available in a location you desire? _____

_____

Related jobs _____

_____

Your Observations

What are the negatives about this job for you? _____

_____

What are the positives about this job for you? _____

_____

(continued)

(continued)

On a scale of 1 to 10, how interested are you in this job in relation to others? _____

What more do need to know about this job before you can make a decision? _____

_____

_____

_____

What barriers do you face in getting this job, and how might you overcome them? _____

_____

_____

_____

Would you be able to get this job now? If not, what jobs or other experience could you get to help you prepare for this job? _____

_____

_____

What could you do now to begin preparing for this job? _____

_____

_____

_____

Sources of More Career Information

This book has helped you define your career focus. Still, you may wish to learn more about your career choice, explore related career options, or be well-prepared for a future career change. Career research helps you accomplish these goals and more. By doing more career research, you also

- **Increase opportunities in your job search by identifying a wider range of job targets.** With thousands of specialized job titles, you are almost certain to overlook a number of them that would fit your needs very well. Looking up a few job titles is a start, but reviewing more jobs within clusters of similar jobs is likely to help you identify jobs you don't know much about but that would be good ones for you to consider.

- **Find skills from previous jobs to support your present objective.** Look up descriptions for jobs you have had in the past. A careful reading will help you to identify skills you used that can be transferred and used in the new job. Even "minor" jobs can be helpful in this way. For example, if you waited on tables while going to school, you would discover that doing this job requires the ability to work under pressure, deal with customers, work quickly, have good communication, and many other skills. If, for example, you were now looking for a job as an accountant, you can see how transferable skills used in an apparently unrelated past job (such as waiting on tables) can be used to support your ability to do another job.

- **Improve your interviewing skills.** Sure, you may think you know what's involved in a particular job, but that is not the same as preparing for an interview. Most people with substantial education, training, and work experience in a particular field do not do a good job of presenting their skills in the interview. People who do their homework by carefully reading a job description and then mentioning key skills that the job requires in an interview often get job offers over those with better credentials. Why? Because they do a more-convincing job in the interview, and they make it easier for an employer to understand why they should hire this job seeker over another.

- **Find the typical salary range, trends, and other details for jobs.** The descriptions will help you to know what pay range to expect, as well as many other details about the job and trends that are affecting it. But note that your local pay and other details can differ significantly from the national information provided.

- **Write a better resume.** Knowing the specific skills a job requires allows you to focus on those skills in your resume.

The better-prepared job seeker often gets the job over those with better credentials. Remember this, and consider doing more homework on your job options now and throughout your job search.

Major Sources of Job Descriptions and Related Information

While hundreds of sources of career information exist, the books described in this section offer most of what you need. I've listed the primary resource information here. All books are available at most bookstores and libraries or from JIST Publishing at www.jist.com or 1-800-648-JIST.

Occupational Outlook Handbook

If you use only one reference book, this should be it. Published by the Department of Labor and updated every two years, the *OOH* provides more than 270 longer descriptions of the major jobs listed in Chapter 6. Each job narrative includes information on the skills required, pay rates, projections for growth, education and training required, working conditions, advancement opportunities, related jobs, and job-specific sources of additional information, including Web sites. The *OOH* is available in most schools, libraries, career counseling centers, and bookstores. The *OOH* content is available online at www.careeroink.com and www.bls.gov/oco/home.htm.

JIST offers targeted career information based on the *OOH* in its "Top Careers" series. These titles include *Top 300 Careers, 100 Fastest-Growing Careers, Top 100 Careers for College Graduates, Top 100 Careers for People Without a Four-Year Degree,* and *Top 100 Computer and Technical Careers.*

New Guide for Occupational Exploration

The *New Guide for Occupational Exploration,* published by JIST, is the source of the interest areas in Chapters 3 and 6 and the related work groups in Chapter 6. The *GOE's* system of organizing jobs based on interests was developed by the U.S. Department of Labor and has been updated by JIST to reflect the U.S. Department of Education's career clusters that closely link careers and learning. The system was originally based on substantial research into how people can use their interests to explore career and learning options. By grouping jobs together, the system helps people easily find related options.

The *GOE* provides lots of additional information on the interest areas and work groups. For example, the information on each work group includes the types of jobs in that group, the training or education needed, related school subjects, related leisure activities and hobbies, and a list of job titles within each work group. Descriptions for the more than 900 jobs within the various work groups are also included, allowing you to identify very specific careers quickly.

*Occupational Information Network (O*NET)*

This database, maintained by the U.S. Department of Labor, contains specific information on hundreds of data elements for more than 900 job titles. A book titled the *O*NET Dictionary of Occupational Titles* (published by JIST) offers the only complete printed source of the O*NET descriptions. Descriptions include details on related skills, earnings, abilities, education, projected growth, and more. You can access the O*NET job descriptions online at http://online.onetcenter.org/.

Enhanced Occupational Outlook Handbook

The *EOOH* is a good all-in-one reference that includes the job descriptions from the *OOH,* plus descriptions of related jobs from the Department of Labor's O*NET database (about 800 jobs) and from the U.S. Department of Labor's *Dictionary of Occupational Titles* (about 1,700 descriptions). This resource is ideal for in-depth career research because it includes 8,000 job descriptions—more than in any other book.

Best Jobs for the 21st Century

This best-selling book emphasizes jobs with fast growth, high pay, and large numbers of openings. It includes over 500 descriptions plus many useful "best jobs" lists, such as highest paying, best overall, and best at various levels of education. Other books in this series include *200 Best Jobs for College Graduates, 300 Best Jobs Without a Four-Year Degree, 50 Best Jobs for Your Personality, 250 Best Jobs Through Apprenticeships,* and *225 Best Jobs for Baby Boomers.*

Career Guide to Industries

This book by the U.S. Department of Labor reviews trends, jobs, and earnings in major industries, which are listed in Chapter 7. JIST publishes a version of this book titled *40 Best Fields for Your Career.* You can find the industry descriptions online at http://www.bls.gov/oco/cg/home.htm.

Other Helpful Career and Education Books

Other useful books for career and education information include the following titles.

College Majors Handbook with Real Career Paths and Payoffs. This bestselling book by Neeta Fogg, Paul Harrington, and Thomas Harrington is based on an enormous study of 150,000 college graduates. The authors used this information to create a practical guide on the actual jobs and earnings of college graduates in 60 majors. The result is the most accurate facts available on long-term outcomes associated with particular majors.

Quick Guide to College Majors and Careers and *Quick Guide to Career Training in Two Years or Less.* These two guides, by Laurence Shatkin, describe courses of study, related careers, and more in a quick two-page format. An assessment precedes the information to help you determine the best education or training path for you.

Job Seeker's Online Goldmine. Author Janet Wall describes, in a step-by-step format, the most useful, no-charge, noncommercial Web sites and Web tools for career and education information, resumes, job openings, scholarships, and more.

Guide to America's Federal Jobs. This resource by Bruce Maxwell and the Editors at JIST takes you through the federal job-finding process.

Same-Day Resume, 15-Minute Cover Letter, and *Next-Day Job Interview.* These popular guides in JIST's Help in a Hurry series help you find a good job quickly. They are written by yours truly.

CareerOINK.com

The Web site at www.careerOINK.com is operated by JIST to provide a variety of helpful career information resources including

- Quick lookup of jobs in GOE interest areas and work groups and more than 14,000 job descriptions from the *OOH, O*NET,* and *DOT*

- Career self-assessment

- Sample resumes

- Military to civilian job cross-references

Much of the information at careeroink.com is free, although some of the more advanced features require a modest fee.

Other Research Options

You can find career information at libraries, at school career centers, through professional associations (which are listed in the *OOH*), and from people you know who work in jobs that interest you.

The Internet offers a multitude of career sites. Start with the Department of Labor's site at www.bls.gov, which includes access to the job descriptions in the *OOH* and other labor market information. The site at www.jist.com provides helpful free career information, plus a wealth of other resources on career, education, and job search topics.

Index